BARBRO KARLÉN was born i
book, published when she
selling poetry book of all time
years, 9 further volumes of her prose and poetry were
published. She worked as a mounted policewoman for
18 years, and has trained and competed in dressage for
over 30 years. She keeps a horse in Surrey, England, and
visits regularly for training and competitions.

Barbro Karlén, aged 14

AND THE WOLVES HOWLED

FRAGMENTS OF TWO LIFETIMES

BARBRO KARLÉN

CLAIRVIEW
LONDON

*To my dear family, who have always given me
much love and support*

Clairview Books
An imprint of Temple Lodge Publishing
51 Queen Caroline Street
Hammersmith, London W6 9QL

www.clairviewbooks.com

Published by Clairview 2000

Translated from Swedish by Julie Martin

Originally published in German under the title
'... *und die Wölfe heulten*', *Fragmente eines Lebens*
by Perseus Verlag, Basel 1997

© Barbro Karlén and Thomas Meyer 1997

Barbro Karlén asserts the moral right to
be identified as the author of this work

A catalogue record for this book
is available from the British Library

ISBN 1 902636 18 X

Cover by Andrew Morgan Design
Typeset by DP Photosetting, Aylesbury, Bucks.
Printed and bound in Great Britain by
Cromwell Press Limited, Trowbridge, Wilts.

Contents

Plate section
between pages 120 and 121
(Unless otherwise stated, all photos are from
the author's collection © Barbro Karlén.)

Publisher's Note

And the Wolves Howled is the autobiography of Barbro Karlén, the Swedish writer, policewoman, dressage rider and instructor. Her story is told in the third person, under the guise of Sara Carpenter. All the names of the principal players in the drama have likewise been changed, as well as some minor details of the narrative. Karlén's reason for using this literary device was to create a greater objectivity with regard to the traumatic events in her life. Essentially, however, this is her true story.

As a child, Karlén became something of a literary sensation in her native Sweden. Between the ages of 12 and 17, 10 books of her verse and prose were published to widespread acclaim, swiftly becoming bestsellers. In spite of the media fuss that surrounded her, however, only her close family was aware of the young Barbro's inner torment—her dreadful memories of a previous existence on earth. As recounted by Karlén here, from an early age she had powerful recollections of a life as the Jewish girl Anne Frank, who achieved posthumous fame as the author of the famous *Diary*.

Anne Frank is an icon today—a heroine who symbolizes the strength of the human spirit in the face of evil. It is not surprising, therefore, that Barbro Karlén's connection to this historical figure—which she personally experiences as *fact*—has proved problematic to some. Following the first publication of this book in German, both author and publisher came under sustained attack. (See further in the Afterword by the Swiss publisher.) Karlén was of course aware of the possibility of such reactions, and thus the decision to publish these memoirs was not easy for her. The string of events which led her to take the step are described in this book.

Despite the adverse reactions by some people to the original publication of this work, we have decided to publish the English version essentially unchanged. It should be stated clearly, however, that neither author nor publisher seek to cause offence, least of all to those who have been affected in any way by the barbarous Nazi regime of the twentieth century. *And the Wolves Howled* should be taken for what it is: an individual's personal testimony. Yet although personal, it has a universal relevance as one of an increasing number of reincarnation stories which are emerging from around the world today.

SG, January 2000, London

1

Memories from the past

The darkness closes tighter and tighter around her, she is weeping and afraid. Her little body is shaking and she is drenched in sweat. She can hear them running up the stairs, the shouted orders pierce her body like knives. Dogs are barking and with a crash the door is kicked in.

She wakes up. It is almost light outside. The birds are singing and everything is quiet. Still not quite out of her dream she dries away the tears from her face.

She was not yet five years old, but she had been living with these dreams for as long as she could remember. She had tried telling people about what happened to her at night but no one seemed to understand how in some strange way she was living in *two* worlds at the same time. Her parents insisted on calling her Sara, even though her name was really Anne. She thought that was odd. She had often tried to explain to her mother why she didn't respond when they called out 'Sara'. She hadn't got used to her new name yet.

Sara soon realized that it was not natural at all to those around her, like it was to her, to remember the life they had lived on earth before they were born to this one. For her it was quite natural to remember her family from before. She missed her father, whom she loved and looked up to, but whom she hadn't seen for a long time.

To begin with she thought she was perhaps just on a short

visit to the kind people she was living with and who for some strange reason she was supposed to call Mummy and Daddy. But as time went on Sara realized she wasn't Anne any longer and that her father from that life was not going to come and fetch her. She tried to talk to the grown-ups about how weird she thought this was, but she noticed that they just became frightened and that her questions upset them. So she stopped talking about it and kept her questions to herself. It must be a bad thing to remember who you were before, she thought to herself. And as she pushed the memories to the back of her mind, the feeling that she didn't belong in her existence as Sara gradually receded.

But she could not get rid of the dreams. No matter how many years went by, they returned again and again. Almost always with the same fear.

She is trying to hide but is pulled out by a man in uniform. She calls for her father but there is no answer. There is a terrible racket going on. Things are being thrown around the room, furniture is overturned and there are men in uniform everywhere. In her dream she is desperately clutching a book with a red cover, but it is torn from her hands as she is taken away.

Even though she knew that these horrors belonged to another time, she could still not overcome the fear which certain things in everyday life aroused in her: people in uniform, taking a shower, playing hide and seek. Not to mention that to have someone chase her for fun was one of the worst things she could think of. Even though she knew it was a game, she always panicked and began to cry. It was just as embarrassing every time it happened!

Nor could she bring herself to eat certain things—brown

beans for instance. She could remember clearly the strange look her mother had given her when she had told her why she couldn't eat brown beans: 'I really ate myself sick on them last time.' Her mother, who had never offered her daughter brown beans before, had just shaken her head and taken the awful beans away.

Sara herself didn't think there was anything strange about these memories at all; she knew where they came from. But her parents were all the more worried. In the end they were so worried that her mother took Sara to a psychiatrist to see if he could possibly explain her behaviour, which was so peculiar sometimes, to say the least. Her mother wondered whether perhaps she had an imaginary friend she called Anne?

The psychiatrist was none the wiser either. Sara was careful not to say a word about her dreams or about her memories from the life she had had before this one. She knew that he wouldn't understand. Just like all the other grown-ups he would only get irritated and try to silence her. So she was perfectly 'normal' when he talked to her. After the examination he could only say that Sara was just like any other six year-old!

When Sara started school she learned to read and write quickly. Now suddenly a whole new world opened up to her. New and yet familiar. It seemed perfectly natural to write down all the thoughts that went round and round in her head. She woke up at night, got up, sat down and wrote until the early hours of the morning. She wrote poems and stories. And she wrote in her diary, which she could talk to about everything.

She threw away a lot of what she wrote. Not because she

wasn't satisfied with what she had written but because the idea of writing it was just to pour out all the thoughts there were inside her head. The idea that anyone might want to read it never crossed her mind. She liked school and had lots of friends, but she kept her writing to herself.

When Sara was ten years old, her parents took her on a trip round Europe. They were going to visit the big cities like Paris, Brussels and Amsterdam. Paris and Brussels were a bit frightening, she thought, so big and alien. But when they got to Amsterdam she felt as if she had been there before. But she didn't say anything to her parents; they would have been uneasy about her strange ideas.

When they had settled into their hotel, her parents wanted to start by visiting Anne Frank's house. They wanted to see what the place where the Jewish girl had hidden with her parents looked like, and where Anne Frank's diary had been found.

Of course Sara had heard of both the house and the diary, but it had always seemed very strange to her to talk about Anne Frank in school. She couldn't understand how other people also knew that there had been an Anne Frank. And she couldn't bring herself to read the diary they talked about. Sara felt that she wanted her memories left in peace. She wanted to be absolutely sure that she wasn't 'remembering' anything which in fact she had read somewhere.

When her parents were going to ring for a taxi, Sara could not hold her tongue any longer. 'We don't need a taxi at all, it's not far to walk from here.' She was so dead certain that it didn't occur to her parents to object, they just meekly followed her as she walked off.

'We'll soon be there, it's just round the next corner.' Sara herself wasn't at all surprised when they arrived, but her parents stood there speechless and just looked at one another. 'That's strange,' said Sara when they stood in front of the steps up to the house. 'It didn't look like this before.' She looked wonderingly and her parents didn't know what to say.

They entered the house and went up the long narrow staircase. Sara, who had been so carefree when showing them the way, suddenly went quite white in the face. She broke out in a cold sweat and reached for her mother's hand. Her mother was quite horrified when she felt Sara's ice-cold hand in hers. 'But darling Sara, what's the matter?' Her mother stopped and hugged her. 'Don't you want to go in? Shall we go back?' Sara shook her head wordlessly and continued up the stairs hand in hand with her mother.

When they entered the hiding place the same irrational terrors overcame Sara as she had experienced so many times in her dreams. She found it hard to breathe and panic spread through her body. She had to summon every ounce of her will-power so as not to rush out of the room. She felt so cold that she was shaking even though it was high summer, and she couldn't let go of her mother's hand for one second.

When they went into one of the smaller rooms, she suddenly stood still and brightened up a little. She looked at the wall in front of her. 'Look, the pictures of the film stars are still there!'

Her mother stared at the blank wall and couldn't understand this at all. 'What pictures Sara? The wall is bare!' When Sara looked again she saw that this was true. The wall was bare! She felt confused. She knew that the pictures had been there. She had seen them just a second before. But now there was nothing there.

Her mother was so confounded that she felt driven to ask one of the guides whether she knew if there had perhaps been pictures on the wall at one time? Oh yes, they had only been taken down temporarily to be mounted under glass so that they wouldn't be destroyed or stolen. Sara's mother didn't know what to say.

'How in the world could you find your way here first of all, then insist that the steps outside were different and then see the pictures on the wall when they weren't there?' Sara's father was full of questions and really rather irritated. But Sara was quite incapable of saying even a single word. She just wanted to get out of there, she felt that she couldn't stand it a moment longer. She asked to be allowed to go out before her parents and when she promised to wait for them outside they let her go.

Her legs felt like jelly as she went down the stairs. She had never before in her life felt so wretched. The tears ran unrestrainedly down her face, and her legs would not carry her. When she reached the bottom step her legs folded under her and she fell.

For a fraction of a second she saw a man in uniform bending over her. He raised his arm to hit her and Sara instinctively covered her face. When she took her hands away she saw some Japanese tourists standing there looking astonished and staring at her. She got up, embarrassed, and went out into the street. It felt as if she couldn't get enough air. She took long deep breaths and tried to calm herself.

When her parents came out they found her sitting by a tree. She was staring, her eyes red with weeping, at the canal which ran past the house. At first she didn't notice them but when her mother bent down and placed her hand on her arm, she threw herself into her mother's arms. She was so shocked by her experience on the stairs that she tried, sniffing and incoherent, to explain what had happened.

Her parents listened and tried to comfort her but they could not in any way begin to understand Sara's 'memories'. The idea that one might live more than one life was completely alien to them, but after the visit to that house they were obliged to admit that Sara must have been there before. Since they knew for certain that she hadn't been there during *this* life, must it then have been during a *previous* one?

'I don't for one minute believe in that reincarnation nonsense, but I can't deny that you must have been there before.' Sara's father felt very ill-at-ease with what had happened. This was outside the bounds of normality and he didn't like it. He decided not to talk any more about it. But Sara's mother tried to understand and comfort her as well as she could. She hugged her little daughter and held her on her lap until she had stopped crying. 'Sweetheart, I don't know and I can't understand what you have been through, but you never need to be afraid again. I promise you that I shall always be there and always help you. You are the dearest and best thing in my life and I love you above everything else in the universe.' Sara's mother's words caressed her soul and her spirits gradually lifted.

They continued their journey, but the incident in that house was not mentioned any more. Sara's mother tried to bring the subject up again after they got home but Sara calmed her fears by saying that she felt fine and that she wasn't going around thinking about what had happened at all.

This was only partially true. She knew what she had experienced and what horrors she had undergone. But she knew now that it was a time long past, and that there was no danger of her having to go through that horror during this lifetime on earth.

She had no idea then that there were other people from that time alive again too, and that their paths would cross hers once more.

2

'Child prodigy'

Sara continued to write. One day a good friend of the family came to their home and caught sight of a piece of paper lying crumpled up on the floor in her room. He picked it up, smoothed it out and read:

Enmity, hatred and nastiness
are maggots which bite deep,
a big black hole in the heart
which will not heal.

Kill all hatred
and help kindness to live.
Help all good, listen not to evil people,
evil people are maggots
who destroy all the good.

Lies are friends of the maggot,
they bite deep,
kill all lies,
let truth and kindness live.

The friend found more and more poems and stories. There was quite a pile by the time he had finished. 'May I take these and show them to a publishing company?' The friend was full of enthusiasm and Sara let him do as he wished. If she had known then what would come of it, she might have given a different answer.

A few years earlier Sara's parents had divorced. To Sara this was a great sorrow, even though she and her mother had a good life together. She wrote about everything, including of course what it was like to be the child of a divorce:

I came into the world
to a father and mother
as a person
in the land of people
for I am a part of both
father and mother
but even so I am not whole,

I feel I am broken
in body and soul
I feel that I have no hope
I want to be part
of a whole family.
Who was it who said
split up?

I think that mother
and father and child
are one,

I did not ask to have life,
maybe I was an uninvited guest,
but my parents
are nonetheless best,
yet now they each have
a home of their own
whilst I have nothing at all left.

Two half homes
can never become one,
I wish
life had never been mine.

There was one consolation in this misery and that was Sara's horse, her very own horse, Brownie. She had been riding at a riding school for many years and when Brownie, a wonderful mare, was to be sold, Sara's heart had almost broken. And then her mother had bought Brownie as a surprise for her! Sara was of course over the moon about her horse. Brownie was her very best friend and when she was with the horse the thought of her parents' divorce was easier to bear.

It was when she was around seven that Sara's love of horses had really blossomed. She was absolutely fascinated by these marvellous animals. It seemed almost unbelievable to her that such a big heavy animal could move so gracefully. And it was a fantastic experience to be able to control the horse without taking away its natural desire to move. With her horse Sara felt in perfect harmony.

It was soon apparent to Sara that in spite of her size Brownie was a very sensitive and sharp-eared creature, like the wind at the gallop and yet aware of everything around her. Getting close to this creature, being able to offer it love and security, was her greatest joy. Even though she was only eleven years old, she was absolutely certain how important it was always to behave calmly, firmly and with inner strength when she and Brownie were together. The horse had to know that she could always trust Sara no matter what happened.

Shortly after Sara's twelfth birthday something happened which was to change her life almost overnight. The poems which their friend had collected had been accepted by a publishing house and suddenly a published collection of her poems was a reality!

Sara, who wanted to be a child, just like any other, now found herself drawn into a dance which simply whirled faster and faster. Reporters rang up. There was an interview here, another one there. They wanted her on TV, in debating programmes and in entertainment shows. She was suddenly being called a 'child prodigy' everywhere.

If it was possible, the media interest in her grew even more when she decided to write a letter to a well-known professor who spoke on TV about how afraid he was of dying. Sara couldn't help herself, she was just frightfully upset about how such a clever man could sit there on TV and scare people. As a result she wrote the *Letter to the man who was afraid to die.*

I listened to a man on TV for a little while, he said he was afraid of dying. It's just as well that man wasn't as wise when he was born as he is now, because then he would have been afraid of being born as well.

Maybe it wasn't so strange that he should be afraid of dying because this man thought that his whole self was dead for ever when his life on earth was over. I think that it's very unfair to God to think such a stupid thought. He made people so wonderful. We can see, walk, lie down, run, speak, play, laugh, cry, work, be happy or sad, think, wish, travel—we can do so enormously much.

No one here on earth has been able to construct a real person so far. And yet there are people who think that all this disappears in one go. Dear, kind TV-man, you must realize that if we were going to come to an end so very quickly, God wouldn't have needed to create us so precisely. He might as well have made us like tetra-paks which only have to be used once because cardboard is just thrown away anyway.

I would really like to take the TV-man out into the woods and just sit there quietly with him and look and listen to all the wonderful things. See how the small leaves tremble, but it's not because they are afraid for they know that when autumn comes and they fall, they will live again next year and the next and the next. If that little leaf could speak it would probably say something like this: Poor, poor human man who's afraid of dying. I am only a little leaf but I am just so glad we can be beautiful for people every single year. But perhaps people who are afraid can never really see us tiny little leaves who want to be beautiful for people. Perhaps the TV-man doesn't believe God created us at all? So who do you think did create us then?

My father says that he believes in a higher power, but that people developed from just a single cell in the beginning. Mummy would dearly like to believe that there is a life after this one but I am sorry she only *wants* to believe.

Dear sweet TV-man, you're so learned, surely you don't ever need to say on TV again that you are afraid of dying. You must realize that you are frightening half of Sweden. Just think how many people there are who aren't half as learned as you and they must think that everything you say is true. If you happen to read what I write, you would get really mad and say that that child jolly well doesn't understand, and it's true enough that I don't understand a lot but I know that I think you should have talked about what you are educated in and not about something you don't know. I don't think any person needs to pass some great examination to know whether God exists or not. Flowers and trees and animals don't have a school to go to but they are so incredibly grateful every time they wake up to a new life on earth and people surely can't be less intelligent than animals.

Forgive me dear TV-man, but I was cross with you, but I feel much better now. And I just really wanted to tell you that you shouldn't be afraid of dying because you're not just a tetrapak but a lovely person who God has created.

The letter was never intended for publication but when it did come to the knowledge of the media they pounced on it. On news hoardings and front pages they trumpeted: 'Twelve-year-old girl teaches professor a lesson'. 'Well-known professor set right by child prodigy.' Once again the publicity became almost insufferable for Sara. However, when she was invited on to TV to meet the professor face to face, she still accepted quite undaunted. But the professor didn't want to take part. Instead she was interviewed by a reporter and then read her letter aloud. That episode was broadcast again and again in the news and everyone was talking about the girl who had dared to contradict a professor.

The publicity was enormous and Sara felt as if her world was not really her own any more. Of course she wanted to write and of course she was pleased that people seemed to want to read what she wrote, but it involved so much more that she was not pleased about: her friends at school, for instance, who had always been nice to her before. They now seemed to have a growing aversion to her and started calling her names: 'the poet', 'the writer'. 'So you think you're something special do you?'

No, she didn't think she was anything special. Why were they suddenly being so unkind?

After a while Sara realized that it was her writing and all the publicity which had brought about the change, but she could never stop writing, she knew that. It was as important to her as eating and breathing. Her writing and her horse were her comfort in her loneliness. She could always rely on Brownie. When she took her out and rode alone in the woods, it was as if all her cares blew away.

At Uncle Knut's, who owned the stable where Brownie was

kept, she could always be herself. There was no one there who expected her to behave like a 'literary child prodigy'! There Sara had her 'horsy friends', other girls of her own age who also loved horses and didn't care tuppence about whether Sara wrote books or not.

The 'stable' was actually a beautiful old farmstead which the expansion of the city had passed by. It lay like a heavenly island, preserved, with sheltering trees all around. Behind the trees was reality—industries, factories and cars. But Uncle Knut, although he was getting on in years, had fought the powerful developers and even more powerful local politicians to keep his farm. And so far no one had had any success when they had waved bank-notes temptingly in his face!

Sara admired Uncle Knut greatly. She could sit for hours and listen when he talked about the old times. The story of Tricko, a horse which Uncle Knut had once owned, was one she loved. Uncle Knut borrowed horses from the livery foundation; they were horses which could be called up if there were a war. All the farmers who had horses like that wanted real working horses who could draw the plough and do an honest day's work. But Uncle Knut wanted a 'real' horse! One he could both ride *and* use on the land, so he had asked to have a real riding horse. That was Tricko. But the problem was that Tricko absolutely refused to pull the plough, no matter how hard Uncle Knut tried, so in the end he had to give up and send Tricko back.

A few years later Uncle Knut was sitting watching the Olympic games on television. Tricko was there—competing successfully in the Olympic show-jumping class!

'Just think, I had an Olympic horse and I sent it back because it couldn't pull the plough!' Uncle Knut always managed to look as if it was the first time he was telling the story and every time he looked really aggrieved!

Every year for St Lucia all the girls and the one or two boys at the stable had a tradition of putting on a St Lucia procession for Uncle Knut. Very, very early in the morning, on 13 December, they crept in over the crisp snow with their candles and white robes. Beneath the window of the room where Uncle Knut lay asleep they would strike up: 'Night comes on heavy feet ...' to the tune of Santa Lucia. And every year without fail, the window would be opened when they reached the second verse and Uncle Knut, spruced up in a tie and a suit and with his hair neatly combed, would look out and exclaim: 'No, is that you, I would never have dreamt that you'd come.' Then they would be invited into the warm, and the door to the best room, which was otherwise always locked, would be opened. There the table was laid and there was a little Christmas present at each person's place!

Uncle Knut was a very good horseman and he taught Sara a lot about horses and riding. She was always all ears. She learned from the bottom up both how to ride and how to look after horses properly.

Uncle Knut also really understood the art of living and Sara was always filled with the same joy and laughter every time she saw him take a little skip for sheer happiness. It was when he thought no one was looking that he would sometimes skip just for the joy of being. Once when he noticed that Sara had seen him he at first tried to make excuses: 'I'm sure you think I'm not quite right in the head, skipping around like that, an old man like me.' But when he saw Sara's smiling face he added, 'Well so what, maybe it's not so daft anyway; I'm just so happy and that makes my legs quiver and why shouldn't I skip if I feel like it?' Just to confirm it he took another, extra skip to prove that he was right. It made Sara think of Evert Taube's song 'Rönnerdahl'—all that was missing was the garland of flowers in his hair!

There was no let-up in the publicity surrounding Sara and it meant that she received masses of letters from various people. It was impossible for her to read them all herself, so her mother tried to help her. She read the letters, sorted them and gave Sara the ones that needed answering. And Sara tried to answer them, although it took up a lot of her time. But she didn't feel that she could leave all the people who wrote to her with such warmth and love waiting in vain for an answer. There were young and old, healthy and sick, unhappy and happy people who wrote to her.

But when her mother passed over a letter and said it was from a German man living in Sweden, Sara signalled an abrupt halt. 'I can't write to him.' Sara felt an irrational reluctance and her mother realized that there was no sense in persisting. But Sara's mother, who had read the letter and had been moved by the German man's story, decided to answer him herself. This led to their beginning a correspondence and after a while they also began to meet.

Finally Sara's mother asked her to go with her and meet Erwin Kramer, as the man was called. For her mother's sake Sara agreed but she felt incredibly ill at ease at the prospect of the meeting. She said nothing to her mother, who was delighted that Sara would finally meet Erwin.

In spite of Sara's reluctance, after the meeting she was obliged to admit to herself that the man her mother had introduced her to was very kind and unusual. Erwin, who was an artist, had fled from Germany to Sweden in the middle of that terrible war. On a raft, with three friends, he had risked his life to get away. It was in the middle of winter and their chances of survival had been slim. But when things had looked darkest and the men on the raft had been exhausted with thirst and cold, help had come from 'above'! They had been picked up by a Swedish fishing boat which took them to Sweden and safety.

Erwin told Sara how he had been forced to leave the country. He was forced to leave his brothers, sisters and parents to get away from the war. For him it had been absolutely unthinkable to go out and fight for Hitler. His only way out had been to flee. Sara had listened and understood that Erwin was a very special person. His story of how he had fled, how terrified he had been of being captured by the Germans, his own people, moved Sara deeply. She felt a kind of bond with Erwin after that.

Sara's mother and Erwin continued to meet and after a couple of years they moved in together. Now Sara had two fathers and she didn't have anything against it. Erwin was a real 'dream father'. He always had time for Sara when she wanted to talk and her mother seemed much happier than she had been for a long time.

Sara, who was now thirteen, still found happiness in her writing. She still only really wrote for herself, but since a lot of people evidently wanted to read what she wrote and the publishers who had published the first book were putting pressure on her, she agreed to her work being published. Over the next four years one or two books were brought out each year. They all dealt with the same subject: with the love of animals, nature and people. And with good being strong, with the fact that good always conquers in the end.

Sara found a lot of her inspiration when she went out walking alone in the countryside or strolled by the sea. She sought solitude more and more frequently. Then she was able to sense how nature flowed through her whole body. It felt like brilliantly coloured waves. When she walked by the sea at sunset, alone and with bare feet, the murmur of the sea sounded like musical harmonies. She wondered what the forces were which gave her the ability to write.

The words came to her in torrents, they cascaded through her brain and she just had to hold the pen. Sometimes when she was writing they came so quickly that she could hardly keep up. It was a wonderful feeling when the words poured from the pen without her needing to think for one second about what she should write.

It was Sara's wish that what she wrote should help people to understand how they should live in harmony with nature, animals and themselves. She wanted to tell people that there was no death. That everyone, without exception, was born again and again. She wanted to give people comfort and confidence. And she wanted to tell them that there was no avenging God, no God sitting on a throne and judging people. That they judged themselves.

'As ye sow, so shall ye reap,' it said in the Bible. It could not be put more simply. Sara knew that the world's wars, greed, thirst for power and evil were the consequences of people being lost and ignorant. If people knew that they were born again and again and that you had to reap what you yourself sowed, the world would look different, Sara was quite convinced of that.

She thought a lot about the opposition between good and evil. In her books she often described the most beautiful of all worlds. Like in *A moment in the Flower Kingdom*:

'I remember the first time I really thought deeply. It was just before I started school. Some of my friends and I were on the seashore. The huge, unfathomable ocean lay before us. Rocks, sandy beaches, stones, washed up bits of driftwood, gulls circling over the water and the occasional swallow or sparrow passing by as part of the universe.

I wanted to explain why I quite suddenly realized that perhaps I was different. I felt that I was at one with nature, with the universe, at one with the great wonderful world which just was there. An enormous feeling of happiness suddenly welled up in me. One of the girls said, 'Shouldn't we go home, it's no fun any more.'

It took only a moment before I walked away from the other girls, I felt that I couldn't go with them. 'No fun any more'. How could she say that? I began to wonder what it was due to. Couldn't she see the mighty ocean, the blue sky with the fluffy clouds, the gulls' proud flight. Or the little shellfish which had been tossed up on the beach. Or the wet sand which had small crests like little waves.

Surely everything had its own story to tell. I remember how I sat down, alone on the beach. I experienced the minutes of eternity. It felt as if the whole of nature was giving me its innermost self. The lapping of the waves was just like the beating of my own heart. The little shellfish lay just by my feet; I got up, took it and put it back in the water, back in its own world. I took a handful of the wet sand, talked to the grains of sand, felt that they too were at one with everything. I felt peace, love, communion with everything.

The sun began to sink, all the colours blended together—the sun, the sky, the sea. Everything, everything became one. I, a little human ant, was part of this unimaginably beautiful story. I remember that I looked around me, looked, felt, lived. Felt that I was a part of everything. I had bare feet, felt the wet sand under them, felt the earth's own warm life beneath. I walked along the beach, it felt as if I were on a walk around the whole earth. It felt as if I was looking for something. But what was there to look for? I had found everything in a single great incomprehensible eternal present. Could beauty get bigger and more beautiful? Could peace be more complete?

No, but I will tell you what I was looking for. There was a yearning which came upon me suddenly. It just was there, inside the whole of me. It was in my head, in my heart, in the whole of me, in my hands, in my feet. I was looking for someone whom I could share all my experiences with, someone who could come to me as the whole of nature had come to me.

I felt myself divorced from the human world. I remember how my thoughts took shape. How I understood that it was a huge unfathomable gift which I had been given, to be allowed to open my senses to all unearthly beauty. I felt how I became conscious of higher worlds where everyone could live in peace and beauty. Where everyone could see true life.

I heard a voice which came to me from space, like music. It was as if the voice said: 'You, little earth child—there are many mansions with our Father. In those mansions beauty never vanishes. Some human children can already catch glimpses of that beauty on earth, just as you have seen and experienced. The musical voice from space told of the Kingdom of Flowers, of innumerable beautiful worlds.

I promised the voice on the beach that I would write the story of the Kingdom of Flowers one day. Write about all the beauty, all the life, all the experiences which came to me.

But always, always I looked for someone to share my thoughts with. I always felt as if I was constantly on a quest, always expected to find another wanderer who spoke the same language as I did. I knew that there would be one. I felt it inside myself. I searched in the skies of heaven, in the stars, in the sea, in the wind, I searched everywhere.

Shall I tell you where I found what I was looking for? I found it on the ground. Footprints. Footprints of bare feet. Footprints which had trodden on the beach. Someone else who was also out wandering, who was looking. The footprints became clearer and clearer. They were almost fresh footprints. It couldn't have been long since the wanderer made them. Now I had caught up with the wanderer who had gone before me. Suddenly I could see him towards the horizon. He was waiting for me. He had heard the sound of my footsteps, he'd stopped, he was waiting.

For a long moment we just looked at one another. Wordlessly, quietly, reverently. It was as if the whole of nature was holding its breath. The being standing before me was Everything I had looked for. This was the one I had looked for and waited for. He could tell me about everything beyond the hosts of stars on the Milky Way, behind the ocean's unfathomable songs, beyond the eternal longing in a human heart. He could tell stories about the beauty of the worlds, He offered security and peace to a little earthly creature. He told me that He had always been there, that He had always left footprints behind. He promised me that I would be able to feel His nearness at any time. 'Perhaps I am not always visible to people when I come close to you, but I shall always be in you and with you.'

I began once again to be conscious of time. I felt how the world, the people's world, was coming back. Dazedly I looked around. The One who had come from Nowhere was gone. But gone only from my outer sight. Inside me He was there. I looked up. The last golden red rays of the sun painted a wonderfully beautiful picture for both my outer and inner sight.

But Sara also wrote about the absolute evil which she knew, for example in *A moment in the depths of the abyss*:

One day Evil sent a messenger to the human earth. He sent many thousands of evil spirits to earth to ask whether anyone wanted to be as strong and great as the devil himself. But although people were evil there was no one who dared to be as wicked as that.

When the terrible spirits had almost given up hope, a cold hard voice was heard calling out into space: 'Here, come here, come here to me, I will arrange the devil's war.' All the evil spirits straight away hurried towards the place where the voice was coming from. The spirits found a man who looked kind and good to their way of thinking. But the man was horrible and wicked.

'What's your name?' said the first evil spirit who arrived. 'I'll give you three guesses' answered the man. 'Is your name Fear?' he asked. 'No,' said the man. The second spirit guessed that the man was called Slaughterer. 'No,' said the man. 'Well then, I know you're called Torturer.'

When the fourth evil spirit was about to guess, the man was filled with laughter. The spirit said: 'You called out to us who are lords over all evil, "Come here, come here," and when we come you just stand there and smile, do you think that's right?' 'You just said my name' said the man. 'I called out "*Here*" (Swedish: *hit*) and then I *smile* (Swedish: *ler*), that makes H-i-t-l-e-r.'

Now all the spirits laughed at themselves, it was so simple, of course it made Hitler. 'You'll get a different name from us,' said the evil spirits. 'You shall be called the "Wild Beast". You shall kill all the people who don't want to obey you, for you shall be allowed to borrow the devil's power. So you shall make war over all the human earth. There is a people called the Jews, those you shall destroy and kill.'

'Can I do all this alone?' wondered the man who was called Hitler. 'No, you shall have help from many, many other evil people.' 'Well that's good, because otherwise I wouldn't be able to do it. There have been lots of wars, but nobody has ever managed to win the whole earth.' 'Just do as we say, Wild Beast, and you will manage it. Just don't forget that first all the Jews must go.'

And so that is how the terrible war began. It was dreadful. Nothing but death and blood and starvation and suffering. And all the evil spirits in the devil's kingdom were happy. 'Now we shall soon have all power,' they said. It just got worse and worse. Anyone who was in the war can tell you about it, the pen can't. The Jews were not allowed to walk or stand anywhere without the police watching over them; they hadn't begun to kill them yet.

But it wasn't long before the fighting men received orders to kill as many Jews as possible, both in their own country and in other countries. They built huge ovens to burn the Jews. All Jews had to bear a mark so that people could see which ones they were.

In a country close to the Wild Beast's country lived a Jewish family which hid in an annexe. There was a long staircase leading up to their hiding place. It was gloomy and dark and creepy but it was a lot better than being burned alive by the Hitler people.

To begin with it was a bit strange for the family, but they quickly got used to it. The hours became days, the days became weeks, the weeks became months and the months became years. And the family managed to hide.

The youngest daughter of the family wrote a diary and recorded all the dreadful things that happened. It was not just the war that the little girl was grieving for. Her mother neither could nor would understand her, but it didn't matter too much; the girl had her father and her diary. Outside, the war was raging; how long could they hide? People were dying outside but in the annexe there was just their hopeless everyday life. Would they ever see the blue sky again?

There was a little hole in one wall where the little girl crept in and looked at the stars sometimes. Wonderful stars which gave the child joy. Every moment the family were in tremendous despair, wondering when the soldiers would find them. The guns thundered and the whole world was shaking with fear. The little Jewish girl went up all alone to the attic and prayed to God. The little one got her whole strength from Him.

'Dear God let us survive,' she prayed. 'I want to work for good, help me if it be your will.' But perhaps it was not God's will. Perhaps He wanted the little girl to get away from the evil earth. Policemen came and forced their way into the annexe. The little girl was taken away by evil policemen to the war country, to a place of death. They tortured her and wanted her to do terrible things. The little one couldn't even cry. Her eyes were dry as a desert but she had her comfort in God.

One day when she was working together with other Jews, both young and old, the little girl said she was cold. A policeman heard what she said and straight away he took her by the arm and dragged her to a great oven and said, 'Now you'll be sure to get warm, you wretched little Jewish cat.' And he threw the little girl into the burning oven. But God held his hands around the little girl's body, so she was not burned at all.

They did the same with many, many others and the war just went on. Every day was a feast day in the kingdom of the devil.

The media interest in Sara did not diminish and the publishing house published one book after another. Sara's mother tried as best she could to protect her daughter from the mass media and all their attention. Her mother knew that what Sara wanted most of all, and also what she needed, was to be left in peace for a bit. Sara wanted peace and quiet. She wanted to be with her horse and she wanted to be like any other ordinary child.

School became more and more unbearable. Her schoolmates taunted and teased her every day. And one of the teachers was so infuriated by her books that he told her she should not imagine that she would get the top marks in his subject, Swedish, just because she had written a few books. She hadn't expected it either. But she had had full marks in all his tests, so she couldn't understand why she should be punished because what she wrote was published? She didn't dare say anything to him when she got her report and the mark was low.

But she was very surprised when one day the teacher came with a bundle of papers and gave it to her. They were poems which his daughter had written. He had on several occasions complained to Sara that his daughter also wrote poems but that no publishing house wanted to publish them. He didn't think Sara's poems were better at all. When he handed the poems to Sara he said that she should take them to her publishing house and see to it that they were published. Sara didn't know what to say. It was terribly awkward. She looked up at her teacher who was standing there with a superior smile on his lips. She tried frantically to find a good excuse for saying no. But she couldn't and she just stood there silently with the bundle of papers in her hands.

'I expect you to let me know how you get on as soon as possible.' Pride shone from his eyes and he stood a little taller when he turned and went. Sara stood there quite bewildered. 'Wait.' He turned around, surprised, when she called. She went with firm steps towards him and pressed the poems into his hands. She said nothing but she gave him a long, considering look before she turned and walked away.

The next year she got an even lower mark in Swedish. But it was not only the teachers who had begun to behave strangely. The schoolmates who teased and tormented her the worst on normal days were the first to come forward and claim to be her friends when the TV or the newspapers came to get a story. Why, why on earth were people so false? Either you liked someone and were their friend or you didn't, surely? Sara pondered a lot about why people were so strange.

One day Sara was sought out by a classmate. He was one of the very worst at tormenting her in the schoolyard in the daytime. Now he told her that she should write an essay for him, which he didn't feel like doing himself but which they had been given as homework. Sara tried to explain that she couldn't do that and that it would not work in any case. The teachers knew exactly how their pupils wrote. They would see through the whole thing and then there would be problems.

It almost seemed as though he understood. He said, 'Cheers,' and went.

The next day, as Sara crossed the schoolyard, she heard someone calling her. She stopped and turned. At that moment a stone hit her on the temple. Sara couldn't remember anything more, she was unconscious and was taken to hospital in an ambulance. She drifted as if in a fog. It didn't hurt at all but she didn't really know where she was.

The picture becomes clearer and clearer. Suddenly she realizes where she is. She is back with her real family. There's masses of beautiful furniture and the room is very light. She is sitting on a sofa and talking to her father. They are whispering and laughing; she sees her mother shake her head resignedly and walk out of the room.

In some strange way she is seeing all this 'from the outside', but she knows that it is herself sitting there on the sofa and so close to her father.

'Sara wake up, you must wake up.' Slowly she came back. She didn't want to leave the room and her father, but she was drawn inexorably back to reality and the present. When she opened her eyes she saw her anxious parents, and her mother hugged her. 'Thank God, thank God, you have been unconscious a long while.' Her mother dried her tears; she had cried her eyes out. Sara remembered her 'dream' quite clearly, but she didn't tell anyone what she had experienced.

3

Happiness—and harsh reality

Sara continued her schooling, but the torment grew greater and greater. She suffered agonies every day. The bullying increased as time went on and when she had at last completed her final year, it felt as though she never wanted to set foot in a school again.

She had only one thought in her head and that was to get away from all people. She had her true friends among the animals and in nature. She wanted peace and quiet, she wanted to be alone. Her dream was to be able to live on a farm with her animals. Perhaps the dream could become a reality if she took the money she had earned from her books?

She began to study the small ads pages in the papers. And after a while the dream house turned up. One grey, cold and snowy January day Sara came to Woodland Cottage for the first time. Buried in its snowy winter garb the little farmstead lay far out in the forest. The frosty winter morning sun was trying to push through the mists. Sara stood as if spellbound. The house was on a small rise, with a barn on one side and a little chicken coop on the other. It had two floors; it had a broken roof and was built entirely of wood. Sara thought it was absolutely perfect and she couldn't conceal her enthusiasm from the agent. Woodland Cottage was everything she could ever have dreamt of. 'This is where I want to live and I shall be able to write here,' she thought to herself when she went round with the agent. Sara knew that she had found her home.

A few weeks later everything was ready; Sara left the big city and her parental home. Sixteen years old in a cottage in the forest. There were plenty of people who raised their eyebrows and thought it was extremely odd. But her mother and Erwin understood her only too well. They had after all seen how the reporters and others had almost driven their daughter out of her mind. Not that these people had wanted to damage her. No, rather the reverse, but the attention had been so intense that now what Sara needed above all was to be by herself.

And that she could at Woodland Cottage. In fact she wasn't really alone at all! She had Brownie, two dogs, Jackie and Donna, two cats, Selma and Alma, one sheep, Woolly-Anna, and masses of hens and chicks. And not to be forgotten, the two cocks, Jack-the-Wimp and Genghis.

Here she could be in peace and here she could write. Sometimes she had a visit from her mother and Erwin, but mostly she lived alone with her beloved animals. And she was happy. She could live close to nature and close to her friends, without masses of demands to be this, that or the other thing.

The freedom she experienced when she walked barefoot out into the dew-wet grass and, with just her night-dress on, jumped up on Brownie's back and galloped away over the meadows with Jackie and Donna leaping happily around the horse was absolutely indescribable.

The happiness she felt when Alma came proudly bearing four small red-brown-grey-white kitten bundles to show her was almost incomprehensible.

The lamb, Woolly-Anna, whom she had fed with a bottle and who had grown into a big sheep, was still convinced that Sara was her mother and followed her everywhere, which was a nuisance sometimes, but even that was part of Sara's new found harmony.

The chicken run. Going out every morning and fetching the eggs for breakfast, against the protests of the laying hen who had determined that all the eggs laid belonged to her and not Sara, was an experience every time. And the eggs which did not become breakfast eggs turned into chicks, to the hens' and Sara's great delight: little yellow and brown balls of fluff which cheeped incessantly and always wanted to go off exploring outside the chicken run.

The two cocks were constantly competing for the hens' favour and it was always Genghis, the biggest and meanest of the two, who carried off the honours. That went on until the day when Sara could no longer stand seeing Jack-the-Wimp always defeated. Determinedly she captured the poor, faint-hearted, colourless cockerel. She put him down on the kitchen table and painted him with water colours in all the colours of the rainbow. She looked proudly at her handiwork when she had finished, and Jack-the-Wimp was let out into the chicken run again. All activity stopped. The hens stared and Genghis couldn't even bring himself to attack the colourful intruder! The next few days were probably Jack's happiest; all the hens made a fuss of him and Genghis didn't dare protest! But what happiness lasts for ever? The first time it rained Jack-the-Wimp's happy days became just a memory and everything went back to normal. Until Sara painted him again!

For the first time in what was now seventeen years of life Sara was altogether happy. She had been allowed to leave school behind her. The dreadful dreams which had followed her throughout her childhood had more or less gone and she was spared all the attention. On Brownie's back, with her food bag, paper and a pen, Sara rode out on long hacks. Alone with her horse and her dogs, out in the wild Sara found the peace and inspiration she had so desperately longed for. She wrote and she wrote. Never before had the words flowed so freely and never before had she felt so free.

'My golden town'

I flee from noise, town smells and houses
I flee to God's country so free
I am lulled to sleep by the murmur of trees
A lullaby hummed in a major key
I feel my freedom in every limb
I feel so glitteringly glad
Nature the free is my childhood home
and the forest my golden town

My town has streets of the softest earth
Stress is prohibited here
My town doesn't know about VAT and the tax
My town is still freedom's sphere

You don't need money to be let in
Here freedom's laws still reign
Here are friends big and small
Here the strong help the weak.

Naturally Sara was not alone all the time. She had friends who sometimes came to call. One of them, Ralph, was rather special. Ralph was a law student and seven years older than Sara. He had come to Woodland Cottage with one of Sara's cousins on a visit. Ralph was tall and good-looking and he radiated a gentle peacefulness which gave Sara a feeling of security. He could talk about serious things just as much as he could get her to laugh uncontrollably, and he could persuade her not to take things so seriously. With Ralph Sara felt that she could be entirely herself. He understood her love of animals and her need sometimes to be by herself and write. He also shared her love of Woodland Cottage and of nature.

Sara became totally absorbed by the feelings she had for Ralph and in the middle of summer in the year she reached 18, they were married. The wedding took place in a little early nineteenth-century church, and all Sara's friends were there.

She couldn't really grasp her enormous happiness! She, Sara, was loved by the world's most wonderful man and their love would last their whole lives through. When after a few months she also realized that they were to have a child her happiness knew no bounds. For the first time in her life Sara wrote a love poem:

'Let me feel your hand'

Let me feel your hand
and be flooded with faith
let me find your eyes
and feel the freedom they offer
Let me rest in your arms and sense the timelessness
Let my soul fuse together
with your soul
in a wordless communion
Let us keep our love alive
through the small everyday things
and the great exalted things
will follow on close
in the same tide.

Sara began to plan for her little family; she saw the whole world in a rosy glow. In all her happiness and naivety she didn't see the signs. The signs a more experienced woman would have noticed immediately.

Ralph had more and more to do, he didn't manage to spend so much time at home. He had to travel, etc. The excuses were many and transparent, but Sara was still living in her little rosy world and believed in 'everlasting' love.

Reality hit her with devastating force. Ralph was away from home as usual and Sara decided to drive to Ellen, one of her friends who lived not far from Woodland Cottage. It might be nice to have a little chat with Ellen and show her how her tummy was growing, thought Sara, who was in a happy mood as she drove off.

Nobody opened the door when she knocked, so she went in. People didn't lock their doors in the country. 'Hello, anyone home?' No answer, so Sara went on into the house.

In less than a minute the bitter truth was thrown in Sara's unsuspecting face. When she left the house she was no longer the trusting girl who saw life through a rosy haze. Deceit and treachery were suddenly a reality. She walked to the car as if in a trance and drove home. The sight which had met her eyes behind the closed door would be imprinted in her mind for the rest of her life, that she knew.

What had she done to drive Ralph into the arms of another woman? Sara blamed herself because she must have done something wrong. Had she not been loving enough? She was six months pregnant and had begun to feel more tired and perhaps she wasn't so attractive? Had she driven him away? Why? How could he? Sara thought she would go mad with all the questions which were whirling round in her head and which she knew she would never find an answer to.

When she came home she resolutely began to put all Ralph's clothes together, and when he rushed in through the door a bit later Sara seemed quite calm although her soul was in tumult. She handed him his clothes without a word.

When Ralph tried to explain, Sara heard herself say that she wanted a divorce as quickly as possible. She knew that it was too late for her and Ralph. There were no explanations that could change anything. Ralph did not protest and left her saying that if there was anything she wanted she could contact him at Ellen's.

Disillusioned, but with her feet considerably more firmly on the ground, Sara lived through the last three months of her pregnancy. Her mother and Erwin came to Woodland Cottage and stayed with her. Sara felt as if they were her lifeline and her only security.

Early one morning in the middle of May Sara's son came into the world. A well-formed lively little creature who brought Sara a happiness which she had never thought possible. With little Martin in her arms her belief that there was a meaning in everything that happened was confirmed. Even if things sometimes seemed impossible and dark as night, something good came out of it in any case, that was Sara's philosophy. She was unendingly grateful for the way everything had worked out for her to have Martin. Even towards Ralph Sara felt great gratitude; without him her son would never have been born.

So she felt nothing against either Ralph or Ellen. But when the two of them came up to the hospital hand in hand and gave her a bunch of flowers, Sara didn't know whether to laugh or cry! As luck would have it they left again before she had decided which.

Sara and little Martin were allowed home to Woodland Cottage after a few days and there the new grandmother and 'grandad' Erwin were waiting. Spring became summer and Sara enjoyed every minute of her wonderful son. She thought life wasn't so bad after all in spite of everything, but reality had only just begun.

One day a buff envelope arrived from the Inland Revenue. 'The property is to be sold...'

Sara read the letter over and over again. It said that Woodland Cottage would be sold if she didn't immediately pay the tax which the state claimed she owed. She couldn't understand it at all. Surely there was some mistake? She had consulted a tax consultant a long time previously who had promised her that he would take care of her tax demand, which was so obviously wrong. At any rate that was what he had said when Sara had talked to him. She hadn't even earned as much money as the state was now asking her to pay. The consultant hadn't been a bit concerned when he took over her case and he'd said that it was just a formality.

Sara read on: 'Since no appeal has been lodged within the appointed term, the tax demand is upheld and is thus due for payment within thirty days.'

When Sara put down the receiver a few minutes later after speaking to the tax adviser's secretary, she sank defeated into a chair. What was it the woman had said when Sara had asked to speak to him? 'I'm afraid he's dead. He died three weeks ago.' The tax consultant who was to have helped her show the Inland Revenue that the tax demand was completely wrong had died. All his cases had just been left, Sara had learned from his secretary. Now it was too late to do anything.

Sara tried day after day to ring, write and speak in person to someone in the Inland Revenue who could tell her what to do to get this crazy ruling overturned. But she was just passed from one to another. Nobody wanted to know anything about the 'case' as it was called. The days passed quickly and fearfully. Sara realized that she would be obliged to sell Woodland Cottage before the state simply took it. If she sold the little farm herself there was a small chance that she could pay the tax and perhaps have a little left. But if the state took the farm it would be auctioned and then there was no certainty at all that it would even cover the tax demand.

Woodland Cottage proved easy to sell. The first prospective buyer made up his mind immediately and before Sara could really grasp what was happening Woodland Cottage was no longer hers. The tax demand was paid by Sara in the hope that she would win her case against the state in the future and get her money back. But she would never get Woodland Cottage back. When this finally sank in fully, she had to exert all her strength to keep a grip on her life at all.

One raw and cloudy day in January, Sara and her eight-month old son left their paradise and their refuge. She had had to give away all her animals, apart from Brownie. She wouldn't dream of moving her beloved collies, who had lived so free at Woodland Cottage, to a flat in town. Nor could she contemplate shutting in Alma and Selma so that they could never go out again. No, Sara was obliged not to think of herself, she was the only one who would have been happy if she had been able to take them with her. But she just couldn't get rid of Brownie. She couldn't really afford to take her with her to town and have her on livery in a stable; it was going to cost several thousand crowns a month. But how could she possibly sell her Brownie?

Sara's mother had arranged a flat in the old manor house where she and Erwin lived. In itself it was a charming old wooden house comprising about ten flats and located almost in the centre of town. The flat was large and roomy but Sara's heart wept for Woodland Cottage. For the freedom, the silence and the peacefulness, for the countryside and the animals.

The small sum of money which was left from the sale of Woodland Cottage was soon used up. Sara realized with increasing despair that there was no room for Brownie and her expenses in the budget. Without work or training and with a very modest income from the books there was no other choice than to sell Brownie.

It was not until Brownie went off in the horse-box to her new owner that Sara really realized what she had done. She had sold her best friend for money. That fact was far more painful for her than that she could never again ride her beloved horse. Sara felt as if she could never be happy again.

Alone with her son and with no possibility of earning any money before she had some further education, Sara finally felt compelled to try and get help from the authorities. The authorities who had so readily taken her taxes since she was twelve years old, and who had made sure she was obliged to sell her home. So far she had never either asked for or got a single penny from the state, but now perhaps it was time?

Sara took Martin in her arms and went into a social welfare office. She soon learned that she couldn't expect any help from them. 'You're an author and self-employed so you must have money stashed away somewhere! People like you can't come in here and get money, whatever you may think.' The welfare assistant glared angrily at her. Sara said she was sorry but she had no money. 'Are you a drug addict?' 'No, of course not.' Sara was almost shocked by the question. 'Come back when you are!' That was the end of the conversation.

One experience the richer and many illusions the poorer, Sara realized that she could not expect any help from the authorities. She had hoped and believed that she would be able to get help to get on her feet again. She lived exclusively off her mother and Erwin. Without their help she would have ended up on the streets with her son.

Trying to pay her way by writing books was absolutely hopeless, Sara realized that. If she managed to sell what she wrote, there would still be more to pay in taxes than she earned. The only option was to go back to school to try and study for the exams she needed to get into some form of higher education. Medical studies for example, which she had always dreamt of, but which for various reasons had never been more than just a dream.

Sara read and studied, borrowed money and tried to juggle her finances and her time. But after a year of studying it wouldn't work any longer. She realized that she absolutely had to start earning money instead of borrowing. And she now knew that she would never get back the tax which she had paid; the tax inspector she had spoken to had made that absolutely clear to her. It didn't matter how hard she tried to explain and show him how it had happened. The time for appeal had expired. That was that. The money was and would remain confiscated.

Sara thought long and hard about what she should do. Finally she had made up her mind.

4

In uniform

Her choice might seem strange, but there were three reasons why she decided on a profession which was so far removed from her character:

Her irrational fear of uniforms had not diminished with the years, rather the reverse. In fact it was a lot worse now than when she was young. Now she was an adult and expected to act rationally and not panic when a policeman in uniform addressed her. Sara only had to see a policeman in the distance for her heart to start beating faster and for her to start shaking all over. On more than one occasion she had thought of putting her foot down and driving off when she had been stopped at some traffic check-point. So far Sara had always overcome her fear and to some extent also been able to conceal it. But she realized that it was beginning to be a serious problem, which she was obliged to deal with if she didn't want to come to grief one day. She decided that the best way to tackle the problem had to be to confront the 'danger'. If she herself dressed in a uniform perhaps her 'phobia' would go away?

The second reason was the idea of getting paid for riding! The third reason was that she wanted to have an occupation where she knew that she would always have work, and where she was also paid right from the first day of training.

Police work met Sara's three 'requirements'. She decided to concentrate on studying the subjects which she might need to qualify to apply to the Police College. Her mother and Erwin, after their initial shock, promised to help her with Martin.

After an intensive term at the adult education college Sara had her exam results and she submitted her application to the police. A few weeks later she was invited for an interview.

The man who sat opposite her was friendly in a fatherly kind of way. After the 'friendly' questions he then wondered why Sara wanted to join the police. Was it perhaps because as a writer she wanted to write about the police 'from the inside'? 'After all, you have the most dangerous weapon of all, the pen.'

He looked really worried. Sara was somewhat surprised by his obvious anxiety. Was there so much to hide that it justified asking such a question? She assured him that this was absolutely not the reason for her wanting to be a policewoman and with that 'promise' the man looked considerably more reassured.

After the physical tests Sara was told that she had been accepted for the National Police Training.

The fact that much, much later in her life she would be forced to write about her time in the police force was something she could not even have dreamt of then.

One winter's day when Sara was just a little over twenty, she began her 'career' as a policewoman. The college where she was to spend a year was almost three hundred miles from her home town, which meant that she could only go home for the weekends and holidays.

Sara missed Martin so much that her heart ached, but she was absolutely determined to complete her studies and take her exam as a policewoman. She did know that Martin was in the best hands with his grandmother and Erwin.

To begin with it was like any other school, but with the

difference that here there was no one who knew about Sara's background as a writer. She had changed her surname and adopted a name which had been in her family for generations. That was why no one made the connection with the 'literary child prodigy' whom so much had been written about in the papers a few years earlier. That was precisely what Sara wanted and she was careful not to tell anyone at the college about her literary career.

Sara was extremely happy at the college. There was a good spirit of comradeship among the students, the teachers were good and the studies were no problem for her. But she had still not had to try on the uniform or wear it. The first part of the training was mainly theory, with legal subjects, languages, psychology, police matters and of course physical training. But the day for trying on the uniform drew inexorably nearer. She really had tried to prepare herself mentally but she had never imagined that it would be such a terrifying experience.

All her friends, who of course had no idea of her torment, were cheerful and in high spirits. At last they were going to look like 'real' policemen. But Sara was terrified.

She buttoned the shirt and fixed the tie in place with the Velcro fastening. She avoided looking in the mirror. But when she had the jacket on as well, one of her friends enthusiastically held up a mirror for her to see—'See how great you look!'

The panic which hit Sara in that moment was indescribable. She turned away from the mirror image with some excuse to her well-meaning friend. Stinging tears were forming behind her eyelids and she broke into a cold sweat. When she saw the image of herself in uniform it was as if someone had poured a whole bucket of live spiders over her. They crawled over her body, under her hair, into her mouth, nose and ears. Everywhere there were big black hairy spiders crawling over her.

Sara's first instinct was to tear the uniform off and run away. But she talked to herself; time after time she told herself silently, 'They are only clothes. I can take them off whenever I want. Nobody wants to hurt me here. Everything is fine.' After a while she had regained her composure. Everyone was busy trying on their own uniform so no one had noticed her battle with herself. Still shaking, Sara took the white shoulder strap, the cap and finally the truncheon. All around her were her friends, they too in full police regalia. She continued to argue silently with herself and finally she almost managed to look completely unconcerned.

Her time at the college passed quickly. The theoretical assignments were interspersed with practical police exercises and driving. The only subject which Sara did not participate in with any particular pleasure was the physical training! She had never seen the sense in running through the woods and getting completely exhausted, when instead you could walk around with a pad and pencil. Or why not, best of all, ride?

When you ran you neither heard nor saw, you just got tired and sweaty! What was more it was expected that you would participate in games like hockey or weight-lifting competitions for pleasure! No, that was not exactly Sara's cup of tea! Not to mention the terrible idea some sadist had dreamt up: all police trainees had to jump through a hole in the ice in the middle of winter! That was so that they would know what it felt like if at some stage in their future police work they should need to save someone. Sara thought it would be quite enough to experience it then, if she should ever find herself in that situation. But 'voluntarily' to throw oneself into a hole in the ice head first? That was the limit! Luckily enough she had cystitis and a medical certificate to the effect that it was inappropriate for her to get so cold; so to the great chagrin of the instructor there was no ice-bath for Sara!

The comradeship in the class was good and Sara made a lot of friends. She had managed to rent a wonderfully furnished flat as a sub-let, close to the college. This period was, in spite of her missing Martin, a wonderful time. Uncomplicated, easy and character-forming.

Part of her youth, which Sara had lost when she had been pursued at every step by the press and then become a young single mother, she now regained. Here she could go out to parties or hold her own. She went out with her friends and danced. Sometimes on late spring evenings they had picnics in the countryside. At weekends she drove the three hundred miles home to her family. Sometimes her mother and Martin came back with her to spend a week or two.

After one year there was the exam and suddenly the schooldays were at an end. There were a lot of tears shed over having to part from one another but naturally it would be wonderful to be able to be at home again. Everyone thought that it was exciting to begin the 'real' practical training now; one year with the plain clothes criminal police and one year with the uniformed police.

Sara was back in her home town and in her flat with Martin. To begin with she worked in the day, during which time Martin stayed with her mother a few floors up in the same house. Sara was really having a great time. It was interesting to be able to work a few months in the different criminal divisions. Everyone was friendly and helpful and Sara felt that she was well-liked.

That year also passed quickly and it was time for the uniformed police to take over her further training. Once again it was time to put on the uniform but now it was not a torment. Sara had been right to believe that if she confronted her phobia for uniforms it would disappear. Now she hardly thought about it at all, even though she always avoided looking at herself in the mirror when she had her uniform on. She found it hard to reconcile herself with that image, but having people in uniform all around her didn't bother her at all any more. It was an enormous relief.

In the uniformed police she had to work shifts, in other words nights, evenings and days with time off between duties. That gave her more time for Martin, who was now five years old.

The months passed and Sara was more and more convinced that she had made the right choice when she trained for the police force. Most of her colleagues were friendly and helpful. Naturally there were one or two who tried to wind her up because she was new to the work and also a woman. But on the whole that training year passed quickly too, and suddenly she was officially fully trained.

Sara had already realized that you could never be fully trained as a police officer. Every new duty entailed new problems, new risks and new judgements to be made. The really good police officers were those who humbly took on board these fresh lessons and didn't just plod on 'by the book'.

Sara called those other police officers real 'police-policemen'. They were the ones who could never acknowledge that they had made a mistake, or show compassion; who really enjoyed running in people who had perhaps driven a little too fast or forgotten to put the tax disc on the car.

But fortunately these police officers were the exceptions. Most of them were uncomplicated and friendly people in uniform who tried to do the best they could. Sometimes of course it felt hopeless when the car thief you had arrested was back on the street again before you'd even had time to put in your report! And on top of that he might have stolen another car from the police car park!

Now Sara was placed as a radio car officer in one of the suburbs. This was a very instructive period for her even though it was not always particularly pleasant. During this period she had close contact with the other side of society and a very harsh reality. Domestic disturbances. Assault. Suicide. Children who were ill-treated–and much, much more which she would remember for ever.

Sara realized that she was very fortunate. She had had a strong family behind her when she had found herself wiped out and with no hope of coping by herself. That was all that distinguished her from these outcast young mothers in the suburbs, a mother who perhaps had to put up with being abused and humiliated in order to have someone to keep her and her children.

There was so much misery behind the closed doors and Sara often felt helpless because she couldn't do anything about it, apart from perhaps at best solve the particular problem just then.

Having to call an ambulance on Christmas Eve to an abused mother of five children and run the drunken father into the police station and then make sure there was a social worker to take care of the weeping children–these were experiences which marked Sara deeply. Trying to stop a drunken car thief at the risk of her own and others' lives was traumatic for Sara when she realized how close she had come to her own life being wiped out. Finding a young woman at the last moment who had taken tablets to end her life and giving her artificial respiration and cardiac massage, only to learn the next week that she had jumped from the seventh floor, filled her with powerless rage.

Sara was not able to shake off all the misery she had to experience, but nonetheless she felt that sometimes she could make changes for the better for people she met in her role as a police officer. Like the seventeen-year-old girl, a prostitute and an addict, she had sat and talked to for almost the whole night after her evening duty had ended. The girl had come to trust Sara so completely that she had agreed to seek help to get away from her situation. When she visited the girl some time later at a treatment centre and found a young, optimistic and hopeful person looking forward to the life ahead of, instead of behind her, well then Sara felt that she had a role to play in her job.

Here too the atmosphere in the workplace was good; Sara got on well with her colleagues and her superiors. One or two male police officers had views about working with women police officers but usually that sort of opposition was due to the fact that the officer himself was very insecure in his professional role and needed a big strong police officer to hang on to. That kind of officer didn't feel safe in a woman's company because he knew he couldn't cope himself.

On one occasion when Sara came across that kind of officer who refused to drive out with her on duty, she replied that she understood him completely. 'If I had been as little and helpless as you I wouldn't have wanted to drive with a woman either!' That found its mark and after that he never had any more problems with female officers. But usually there weren't any confrontations like that and the work just flowed, and Sara was happy among her colleagues.

She had set her sights on where she wanted to work: with the mounted police, in the Mounted Police Division. Just imagine being able to ride and be close to horses and nature in your working hours! She was convinced that it had to be a dream job.

5

Mounted police

When Sara had completed her training at the Police College she had been offered the chance to look after a horse for a friend. The horse, Bobby, was a big, beautiful, dark grey horse. Her friend had back problems and could no longer ride and instead she asked Sara to take care of Bobby for the time being and perhaps buy him when she could afford it. Sara had accepted with the greatest of joy; she'd been missing horses and riding incredibly. Even though she had sometimes been asked to ride other people's horses, it was not the same as having 'your own' horse and riding every day.

After a while Sara had even been able to buy Bobby, although she paid a very low price. Her friend wanted above all for Bobby to be able to stay with Sara, so she sold him for a symbolic amount. Previously, during Brownie's era, Sara had enjoyed jumping most, but with Bobby she began training for dressage instead. Bobby was a very clever horse with an obvious aptitude for dressage and she had quickly got into competitions with him. They had a lot of success in the highest classes and she dreamt of a place in the national dressage team.

After a while Sara was also elected to a board on which all of Sweden's dressage riders who competed in higher dressage were members. The aim of the association was to promote the welfare of the sport and it was a great honour to sit on the board. Sara was convinced that this, together with her honours from the competitions and her long experience of horses, would be considered an advantage when she applied to the Mounted Police Division. When finally the day came for the riding trial, she was one of the first to register her interest.

She was quickly made aware that in the Mounted Police Division they were not a bit keen on having her or any other woman officer. There were not, and never had been, women officers in that department and that was how it should stay, they thought. As luck would have it the Head of the Mounted Division had realized that they could not prevent it and he himself had nothing against female police officers, provided they were good people and good riders. After a riding trial and an interview Sara was accepted, together with two other women and two male officers.

She loved her new workplace from the first moment. The Mounted Police had a fine old wooden manor house, painted in yellow and white, with a nature reserve on one side, and yet it was close to the centre of town on the other. It was built in a U-shape, with a cobbled yard in the middle. All around the wind whispered through the trees and Sara was met by deer on the first morning when she drove in.

She was so happy her body ached. She thought it was absolutely incredible that she had had the good fortune to get a job in a place like that and together with the creatures she loved most—horses. Sara was so full of joy that it took a while before she realized that the opposition to women police officers had not diminished at all. On the contrary.

The other two female officers, however, were gradually accepted by their male colleagues, perhaps because they were not so used to working with horses and often asked for help. The men were able to show them how to do things and feel like real he-men. But Sara was foolish enough not to ask for help. She could manage perfectly well without, she thought. If she had understood then how she would be made to suffer for that, she might perhaps have acted a little more helpless, so that the men would not have felt she was treading on their toes. But she was happy and naively unaware of how her skill and ability to take care of and ride the horses infuriated some of the male officers. She was absolutely convinced that they would treat her better when they understood that she was not a threat to their existence at all, but perhaps even an asset. Resentment of Sara was not lessened by the fact that she not only had a horse of her own that she was competing successfully with. She also now lived in an absolutely incredibly beautiful house with a fascinating garden, together with Martin, her mother and Erwin. This had not escaped the notice of Sara's colleagues in the Mounted Police. They couldn't understand how Sara, just a normal policewoman, could afford to live in a house like that. Sara couldn't understand it either, she could only see that someone or something had led her to the house because it was evidently meant to be so! The fantastic house should have cost millions of crowns, but it had become Sara's for a price which was almost ludicrous in the circumstances!

The story of how she had got the house was absolutely improbable, but it confirmed Sara's faith in good things and in there always being a meaning in everything that happened.

She had been visiting one of her friends, Maryann. In general Maryann was a very level-headed and friendly person, but on that particular day she had not been her normal self. Maryann had started to have a go at her and criticize her for letting Martin, the poor little thing, grow up in a flat in the middle of town with all the exhaust fumes and other awful things.

She had not relented until Sara had picked up a daily paper and said, half in jest and half in irritation, that of course she would buy a house, if only there was something suitable. She read out, 'Would you like to live in Paradise? Walk in your own parkland and warm yourself in front of a tiled stove in one of the reception rooms?'

The advertisement was huge and it was the first thing you saw when you opened the paper. 'What do you think of that?' Sara looked up when she had finished reading it out. 'Do you think that will be good enough?' For Sara of course the whole thing was just a joke, but Maryann was absolutely serious. 'Let's ring now so that we can go and look at it today.' She was not joking, that was obvious. Sara was absolutely horrified and tried to explain to her friend that it was impossible. She couldn't buy a house, least of all a house like the one described in the advertisement!

But Maryann was as if possessed; she wouldn't give an inch and in the end they were on their way to the house, after talking to the agent. When they saw the house, how it lay so high up on a hill with views as far as the eye could see, they almost fainted. When they came into the house and found one room more beautiful than the next, they could only look at one another speechlessly. It was a completely unbelievable house. Verandas and pillars, leaded stained glass windows and oak fixtures, with fitted cupboards from floor to ceiling.

And there was indeed a real park which you could walk in along the fairly sizeable river which flowed right round the plot! There was a fountain and a little wooden bridge over a pond too. Sara thought she was dreaming when she and Maryann went round with the agent. He was talking the whole time but Sara didn't grasp much of what he was saying; she was completely carried away by the beauty of it all. At the same

time as she was happy to have been allowed in to see such a house, she was saddened. She knew that buying it was beyond all possibilities. She hadn't even asked the price!

'Say you'll take it!' Maryann was completely beside herself. Sara tried to explain that there was absolutely no hope and that it was better they left the house as quickly as possible. She was sad just thinking about it. But Maryann would not give up. 'If you sell your house by the sea, the one you inherited a few years ago, you would at least have the deposit on this one, wouldn't you?' Sara looked at Maryann and saw that her friend was in earnest. The house by the sea? Of course she could sell it, but...?

She began to think about it. Perhaps Maryann was right? They went up to the agent who was now showing the house to other potential buyers.

'What is the price?' Sara tried to sound businesslike but inwardly she was quivering with excitement. When the agent said how much the house would cost Sara realized that yes it was possible. She wouldn't just have the deposit if she sold the holiday house, there would be a little left over! The problem was simply that Sara was not the only one who wanted to buy the house for that reasonable price! And she was evidently the only one who didn't have cash to put on the table. She told the agent that she definitely wanted to buy the house but that first she had to sell her holiday house. He was unable to promise anything since there were so many people interested. When Sara got home she grabbed the telephone and put the holiday house on the market. A few days later the agent rang and told her that Paradise was as good as sold; the contract was to be signed the next day. Sara was completely panic-stricken. She had to do something, but what?

'Go over and see the old lady who owns the house and talk to her, go now.' The words came from Sara's mother and Sara jumped into the car and drove to Paradise, as the area really was called. She had no hope that it would change anything but something compelled her to drive on.

When she swung in to the garden of the house, she met the old lady on her way out. If she had arrived one minute later they would not have met. The house would have been lost to Sara for ever. The lady invited her in and they sat down in the big entrance hall. The kind old lady said she was sorry that unfortunately the house was as good as sold. Everything was ready, it was just the contract that had to be signed.

While they were sitting talking, the old lady looked searchingly at Sara. 'Haven't we met before? You look so familiar to me.' No, Sara could not remember their having met before. 'But wait a moment. Aren't you the one who wrote all those wonderful books? Aren't you the one who was called a literary child prodigy?' The old lady couldn't conceal her joy when Sara, somewhat embarrassed, acknowledged that it was her the lady meant. 'But my dear child, I have all your books! This is absolutely fantastic.' Before Sara could say anything, the old lady had lifted the receiver and phoned the agent. 'I've changed my mind,' Sara heard her say. 'The house is sold to the young lady, Sara Carpenter.'

Sara couldn't believe her ears. When the conversation with the agent ended, the old lady smiled, blinking a little. 'You needn't worry about the money, I'll wait until you've sold your holiday house. You are to have this house and that's the end of it!' Sara's holiday house was sold soon after and the deposit was paid in time. The house in Paradise had become Sara's! So now she lived in this fantastic house and she couldn't fail to notice that some of her colleagues were quite put out by it.

In the evenings when she was not working, she saw to her increasing surprise that her house was very well 'watched'; every evening police cars from the Mounted Police drove past. Slowly, slowly they rolled down the slope which flanked the garden and soon the same police car would come past again, driving slowly up the hill. This went on evening after evening. Sara wondered why they didn't just drive into the yard instead and ring the bell. She would have been more than happy to offer them a cup of coffee but she didn't think she should have to ask them to do her that honour.

At work they made out they had no idea where she lived. Sara realized that it was difficult for them to accept her good fortune in life. The fact that she also had her own horse which she was successfully competing with did not exactly make it easier for them to like her. And there was nothing they could do about it. Instead they began to give her the cold shoulder in the group.

They began to harass her mentally in various ways; one was to get up and walk out of the rest room when she came in. Or to go quiet and look meaningfully at one another if she said anything. Questioning her riding and her skill became increasingly popular. They made sure she had to ride the horses no one else wanted to sit on. They liked talking *about* her but very rarely *to* her.

Sara was tremendously upset about the way she was treated but she refused to give up. She loved her work and her workplace and she knew that she was not the one with the problem, but that it was a few poor police officers who for some reason felt their male identity threatened and who could not accept her.

She spent a lot of time thinking about how she should behave in order not to annoy them as much as she evidently did. Did she need to pretend that she couldn't ride, or would she be forced to move to a smaller, inferior house? The answers to these questions were obvious, but that didn't help Sara in the hopeless situation she now found herself in.

Every year police competitions were arranged in dressage and jumping between the different mounted divisions in the three towns where there were mounted police. Sara was to take part for the first time. She was full of anticipation when she mounted the horse she had been allocated to ride. She had realized that some of her colleagues were very irritated by the fact that she was one of the ones who had been chosen. Just when she had mounted and was about to ride off the window was opened from inside the men's changing room. One of the officers stuck his head out: 'You surely don't think anyone here is rooting for you? We're just hoping you'll fall off and break your neck, you bloody tramp.'

Sara was both shocked and heartbroken, she couldn't think of a word to say but just rode off in silence. On the way to the competition grounds she couldn't hold back the tears. Her thoughts spun round in her head. Maybe she had deserved their attacks? She knew that some people thought she had far too strong a personality, that she sometimes was so self-assured it bordered on the insufferable. But she had really tried to hold back and not get drawn into unnecessary discussions. It was only when it came to the welfare of the horses that she couldn't hold her tongue. She had often regretted it afterwards. Sometimes she spoke home truths that perhaps needn't have been said. Now she determined really to try and hold her tongue in the future.

When she won the first prize in both dressage and jumping only a few people could bring themselves to come and congratulate her. Her colleagues from the other mounted brigades on the other hand were overwhelmingly kind and thought she had done very well indeed, even though she had beaten them.

Naturally not all the officers in her station were jealous and unpleasant. Most of them were actually decent people, but oh so easily influenced. There were actually just two or three who were awful, but they poisoned the whole atmosphere in the Mounted Police. One of them in particular, Ulrich Schmith, seemed to harbour an unreasonable hatred towards her. But for what reason? Sara found it almost hard to breathe when he was close to her. There was something in him which made her feel incredibly ill-at-ease. She felt a contempt, but above all a fear of him which she herself was surprised by. Every time she heard his voice her heart began to beat like a hammer and her stomach turned over. He was constantly criticizing and picking on her. Whatever she did he found fault with. Faults which he was not slow to go round and tell anyone who would listen.

Sara tried to keep away from him as much as she could but at one staff party he suddenly went up to her and started to 'grope' her. He shoved her into one of the offices and locked the door. Then he turned to her with a strange look in his eyes. Sara was absolutely terrified. He held her tight and grinned arrogantly without saying a word. At first she was paralysed with shock when he grabbed her, but then she came to her senses and pushed him away hard and suddenly. She rushed over to the locked door and with trembling fingers managed to unlock it before he reached her. She heard how he swore behind her when she rushed out of the room.

She didn't dare tell anyone what had happened. She was afraid Ulrich would get them to think she had accepted his 'invitation' and she realized that it would bring the whole world down on her if she accused a colleague of attempted rape! She couldn't prove anything after all. The only thing she could do was make sure that she was never alone with him again.

The years passed in the Mounted Police. Things didn't get any better. Sara had more or less got used to a whole lot of whispering going on behind her back. Ulrich just got worse and worse, and he had a few faithful colleagues who backed him up in his harassment of her.

Fortunately the new chief of the Mounted Police—Bill Larsen—was a kind and compassionate man. He had noticed that Ulrich was doing what he could to drive Sara out of the division. He also thought she seemed to be afraid of Ulrich for some reason. He didn't know what had happened but there was something wrong, he couldn't fail to notice that. Bill liked Sara; she was good with the horses and he thought she was a good police officer. He was anxious that she should not lose her grip and give up in the face of Ulrich's attacks. He had little time for Ulrich himself. Ulrich had always had a very unpleasant attitude but Bill had never before seen him behave as he was now doing towards Sara.

'It's not so easy when women invade the men's territory and, what is more, do better than the men, you see.' Bill tried to comfort Sara when he saw her sitting alone and looking sad. Their chats became more and more frequent. More often than not they rode out together, since a system had now been instituted which allowed Sara to ride and work alone. No one dared to take Sara's side, because that would mean risking the same fate—being frozen out of the group.

Thanks to Bill's support, Sara found the strength to continue. She loved the horses and her job after all, and what is more she thought it was both fun and worthwhile to work as a mounted police officer.

As the harassment of Sara increased, so the friendship between her and Bill deepened. They started to see each other in their free time. Bill was divorced and lived alone. He thought it was fun to go along when Sara was training and competing with Bobby.

After a while their platonic relationship gave way to deeper feelings. Sara, who had only had short and sporadic relationships after her failed marriage, felt both trust and security with Bill. He was quite a few years older than Sara but that didn't bother her for a moment. For his part Bill was worried about the reaction of his staff but nonetheless devoted in his love for Sara. He knew that relationships at work were not a good idea, not least between a subordinate and the boss, but it was too late to be wise after the event. He had been able to follow at close hand how some of their colleagues had made life as difficult as possible for Sara. He had also found her alone and in tears all too often.

Sometimes when she had been attacked she had spoken out quite strongly and you could hardly blame her, even though it would perhaps have been wiser to hold her tongue. Bill was not a fighting man; he avoided conflicts as far as he possibly could and sometimes appeared submissive. He couldn't do anything about his love for Sara; he was simply quite determined to show from the start that he could keep his private life and his work quite separate. Nobody would be allowed to get him on that.

He realized that their relationship would upset a lot of people in the department, but they would see that Sara would in no way enjoy any privileges but rather the reverse. If Sara had thought that her persecution could not get any worse, she was quite wrong.

Ulrich hit the roof and was absolutely beside himself. She had rejected him, but with the boss it was fine! His first step was to inform the police chiefs about the relationship. In no circumstances could one stand by and see the boss seduced and wound around the little finger of a subordinate, surely? Sara had to be removed from office immediately otherwise the whole department would leave. Ulrich put forward every conceivable argument to get the police chiefs to take action, and finally Bill was called in for 'questioning'.

He explained calmly and quietly the background to the situation, namely that in actual fact it was because of all the harassment of Sara that they had found one another. He declared that he had tried to take steps against the bullying but that this had only resulted in the staff trying to get him removed from office, with the help of the union. Nor had he received any support from the police chiefs. So he had spent a lot of time with Sara to try and stop her going under as a result of all the persecution and attacks. Now their relationship had developed and they were a couple and he had no intention of changing that. Anyone who didn't like it could always apply to work somewhere else, thought Bill. The threat that the whole department would leave was something he didn't take too seriously. But there was always pressure from Ulrich when he didn't get his own way. The police chiefs contented themselves with grumbling a bit and insisting that Sara must absolutely not enjoy any special advantages.

Bill moved in with Sara and her family. They had become very good friends and it was no problem to them to have a new member of the family. The staff waited and watched. Ulrich did what he could to break them up but never really succeeded.

Bill was a very accommodating boss. He was never impossible when someone wanted to take time off or perhaps to 'slip away' for a while to run some personal errand. But for Sara such favours were unthinkable. 'We can't afford to do that,' was his reply if she asked. Sometimes Sara thought he was unfair, but she understood at the same time Bill's fear of giving Ulrich a single opening to attack.

But outside work Sara and Bill lived very happily together. They shared one great interest—horses. When Sara was taking part in competitions they travelled all over the country. They lived in youth hostels and spent their time with people of like mind, happy and positive people. In the summer they sometimes went out in Sara's little boat, a fifty-year-old wooden dinghy. They would sit peacefully and quietly together for hours on the sea and fish. They enjoyed the stillness and the happiness of being together. Those wonderful times, which were filled with harmony and joy, shut out all the worries and irritations from their workplace.

Sara was still working shifts, but when one of the four police officers who was responsible for training the young horses wanted to retire, the vacancy needed filling. Nobody was interested; the work involved longer hours and less pay, since you didn't get the compensation for unsocial hours. What is more it required a certain degree of skill and interest to take on the young and sometimes somewhat recalcitrant horses. Finally Bill asked Sara if she would like to take on the job.

Sara was overjoyed. The new job meant that she no longer had to work shifts, but simply during the day. That meant that she could live a more normal family life with Martin and Bill. It was just as hard every time to leave the family in the evening or at the weekend—they were free and she had to go to work.

Naturally she would continue to work as a police officer but only on horseback and she would be riding much more. Her work would consist of breaking in and training the horses which she was allocated. When the horses were fully trained after two years they would be put into service with one of the mounted officers working shifts.

Sara tackled her task with enthusiasm and delight. What is more, she really liked Carl Hoffman, the colleague she was to work with. Carl had been more than thirty years in the Mounted Police and would soon be retiring. But until then he and Sara would be working together.

Carl didn't listen to gossip, he said, when Sara asked him if he thought they could work well together. Carl had never done Ulrich's bidding, but he hadn't stood up to be counted either. He minded his own business and looked forward to his retirement. It didn't bother him at all to be told to work with Sara. He respected her for her knowledge of horses and her riding skills. Ulrich tried to get Carl to refuse to work with Sara, but in vain. That made Ulrich absolutely furious and his hatred of her increased daily.

It was four years since Sara and the other women police officers had joined the Mounted Police. More women had come and the men had begun to get used to it. But that didn't mean that the women were fully accepted as equals. There were still some 'macho' police officers who were only too happy to stand by and mock if one of the girls was trying in vain to lift a heavy sack or something like that. The idea that as good colleagues they should help her was absolute anathema to them. The fact that there were also male officers who couldn't lift the sack either was never discussed. Naturally they would help one another!

As a female officer, to try and put forward solutions to problems which arose in conjunction with their work was completely unthinkable. More than once there had been incredibly awkward situations when police riders had been out on duty. On many occasions it was a case of understanding the existing situation and making a quick decision, for example when a large gang of youths had gathered which was both threatening and armed with miscellaneous weapons. In such a situation one of the commanding officers might suddenly turn up and start giving orders without really knowing the situation. If a male officer then objected and explained that there were other and better solutions there was never any problem with losing face or anything like that. On the other hand if a female officer ventured to open her mouth and make a suggestion, it was the end of the world! The most unbelievable abuse could rain down on her. After experiencing this a few times a woman learned not to say a word. Regardless of whether she realized that it would end in disaster, she shut up and did as she was told. Bill was the exception but he was considered soft and unmanly. A boss should definitely not change his mind!

Ulrich's witch hunt against Sara did not diminish. Now it also included Bill of course. A lot of people were surprised at Ulrich's intensive campaign, but it didn't occur to anyone to try and shut him up. But why did he hate Sara so intensely? And what was it that drove him to want to 'eliminate' her at any price? This was what a lot of people were asking themselves.

Everyone could see how Sara was being 'hunted' by Ulrich, but no one lifted as much as a finger to stop him. Even though they did not always share his view, it was much easier to let it seem as if they did. That way they avoided being challenged themselves, with the risk of being excluded. Ulrich was so stubborn in his attacks on Sara that in the end his allegations seemed quite true. It became second nature to the staff to discuss everything she had done or not done. He laid the foundations of a creeping rumour which it was absolutely impossible to stop.

Sara and Carl worked together for just over a year. They got on well together and Ulrich was greatly annoyed. His only chance to get Sara removed from the Division was if she couldn't work together with her colleagues. He'd succeeded with that over the years by taking new officers who had arrived and subjecting them to 'special treatment'. One after the other they had followed his advice and made sure to put in complaints about Sara. Their reward was to be accepted into the group as equals with the other, more senior officers. But he had not succeeded with Carl. Ulrich was delighted as Carl's retirement became imminent.

One day Sara was called in to see Ted Nielsen, the union representative at the Division. Her heart was not particularly light as she sat down to talk to him. She knew all too well which side he was on. The fact that he was involved with the union did not stop him helping Ulrich in his schemes as effectively as possible.

'We're getting a new colleague, and since Carl will soon be retiring, you'll have to work with her.' Ted was about the same age as Sara, but he looked admonishingly at her as if she were a small child. 'You'll have to show a bit of good will, you've been here long enough now so it's only right that you should take care of this new colleague.' Sara realized that there was no room for protest and that Bill had no chance of changing the situation. She felt her stomach turn over as she remembered how other new colleagues had behaved. One colleague she had rode out with never wanted to ride where Sara had suggested and had insisted on other routes. It hadn't mattered to her at all; she had changed her plans. But when that colleague suddenly demanded that she should gallop flat out down steep slopes over rough terrain she had put the brakes on. You didn't put a horse at risk for the 'fun' of careering about in the woods. What was more they were actually police officers in uniform and couldn't behave like naughty pony club kids. She had said so and had abandoned her insubordinate young colleague, whose taunts had followed after her.

Another dreadful situation had arisen when one of the very new girls was to ride with Sara. It had been the first working day after a long weekend, which meant that the young untrained horses had had several days to rest and were naturally full of energy. An important principle of horse training in the police was never to ride among cars and other 'dangers' with a horse which was jumpy with surplus energy.

That morning when they were mounted in the yard, the new young colleague had insisted to Sara that they should ride into the centre to accustom the horses to traffic. Sara had tried to explain that it was not appropriate on that particular day, but that of course they could do it when the horses were rested and calm. The conversation had resulted in her colleague rushing in to Ted, as the union representative, and complaining loudly that Sara refused to go with her to the centre on duty.

Unfortunately this sort of incident was not unusual and Sara realized that they were systematic. It was very clever. They knew that Sara would not negotiate where the horses' wellbeing was concerned. They also knew that she would not lower her standards of professionalism when trying to do as good a job as possible when she was training young horses. That way her hands were tied and people could 'demonstrate' how impossible she was to work with.

Ted had contributed his mite when he and Sara were due to go out and ride round the town on one occasion. Just before they were to leave he asked her if she intended to obey all his orders. She had not understood what he meant, so she had asked him. 'You are to obey all my orders, do you hear me?' he roared. Sara had asked him, 'What orders?' He had answered that for example she might have to stand still with her horse at a crossroads for five hours or more. That depended on how long he wanted her to stand there. She wondered what reason he might have for ordering anything like that and she was told, 'Because it suits me.' She had then asked him if he was in his right mind, and that of course allowed Ted to tell the union that Sara refused to obey orders!

So Sara knew what Ted was up to when he sat there in front of her and with an admonishing look told her that she actually had no choice. She was to work with Rose Lemke, the new colleague who was coming. At the same time as Rose was to start, the two other police officers suddenly stopped training the young horses. They wanted to work shifts and were fed up with all the riding. That meant that Sara and Rose, two female officers, would have to do the same work as had previously been done by four male officers. With the same number of horses to look after and just as much responsibility, but half as many people to do it. It was with unmitigated glee and expectancy that Ulrich looked forward to the imminent disaster.

To begin with Sara noticed that Rose was watchful but not at all unkind or provocative as other new colleagues had been. They rode and worked together day after day. Rose gradually began to question Sara about various incidents she had been told about. Sara was dumbfounded when she heard what rumours were being spread about her. Ulrich was the worst but there were also other officers in the Division. Vernon Stone was Ulrich's best friend and also foreman of the local union branch. Rose made it clear to Sara that he too had been very anxious to tell her 'the truth' about Sara. Now Sara understood why the union had reacted so strongly against Bill when he had tried to protest about the bullying. The fact that people were talking about her and spreading rumours Sara knew, but she was horrified when she heard through Rose just how bad it was. Rose told Sara how she had been looked after for the first few days in the Mounted Police. She had been called into a room where Ulrich, Vernon and Ted were gathered together. There she was told how she should act. 'Whatever she says, you must argue with. Just do everything the opposite of what she wants.' Vernon had been enthusiastic. 'If she can't work with you either, we've got her. Then she'll just have to quit.' Ted had been at least equally keen. 'Of course you know she slept with the boss to get here? Otherwise she would never have been allowed to come here.' Ulrich had given his own detailed version of how Sara had gone about things.

Sara told Rose how things really were. Rose didn't know what to believe. She thought it sounded incredible that grown men, who were also police officers and supposed to stand up for justice and honour, could lie like that. She determined to form her own opinion and not believe either one or the other. But after a while when she heard new stories about what had happened on various occasions when she herself had been present, she realized that Sara had been right. The incidents were distorted and changed till they were unrecognizable and it was always Sara who was to blame for the whole wretched thing. Rose began to see that police officers could indeed tell lies; they were no different from other people. Sometimes perhaps they were even worse?

6

Friends—and enemies

When Ulrich and Vernon realized that Rose had no intention of doing their dirty work, she found out what defying them could mean. Day after day they took her to a little room and had a go at her. They told her one story after another, each worse than the last. 'Sara wasn't really a police officer, she was only there for the fun and the riding.' 'She would never have got in here at all if she hadn't slept with the chief, who had been happily married at the time.' 'Nobody could work with her and what's more she refused to obey orders.'

They all talked over each other and made it quite clear to Rose that if she didn't see sense it would be the worse for her. After every such encounter, Rose would stumble out, eyes red from crying, profoundly shocked. But each time she was that much clearer as to whose side she was on, and she had no intention of giving an inch whatever they threatened her with. Rose believed in Sara. They worked very well together and Rose, who had been used to horses previously, realized that Sara had a very special way with these big animals. She hoped that she could learn more through Sara and what's more they always enjoyed it when they worked together. Never any conflicts or cross words.

Rose had decided to be Sara's friend and workmate, cost what it may. Sara was no longer alone. They stuck together and worked hard to get all their jobs done, several young horses each to break in and train, but also patrolling on their duty horses. It was difficult to get it all done. Even if the four officers who had worked there formerly had not exactly worked themselves into the ground, it was a heavy burden for two.

Sara and Rose, who knew how efficient professional civilian riders were, were astonished at the public extravagance which was totally accepted. However, they realized that it was best to say nothing. Bill didn't even dare contemplate changing the routines. This was how they had always worked and nobody should think they could change it just like that. More than once they were reminded that they were actually in the pay of the state, which meant that they had to do as little as possible for as much money as possible. It was frustrating for Sara and Rose, who saw how small changes could have saved both time and money. But in their exposed position they chose to keep their reforming ideas to themselves.

It wasn't just the new young horses which had to be trained. Sometimes one of the older police horses became disobedient and difficult. It was usually Sara who was asked by Bill to try and sort them out. Naturally this stuck in the craw of the already embittered Ulrich. His hatred for Sara filled his whole world. Everything he said and everything he did was directed against Sara and her existence as a police officer. It was rare for Sara to hear anything from him directly; it came through the 'back door'. She avoided getting in his way as far as she could but sometimes it was unavoidable. If she ventured to speak to him, she laid herself open to a verbal explosion which almost frightened the life out of her.

As Bill now relied more and more on Sara to ride some of the older horses as well, when they needed to mend their ways, Ulrich saw his opportunity. He began to tell everyone who would listen how badly Sara rode and how badly she treated the poor horses. Sara was well aware of Ulrich's campaign but she relied on people using their own eyes to see with. What is more, the alternative for a disobedient and ungovernable police horse was the abattoir, so for Sara there was no other alternative but to try and get it back on the right track again.

Sometimes it was actually dangerous. Some horses had been so totally badly ridden that they couldn't work on duty. The problem was that it was embarrassing for a police officer to admit it when his horse was beginning to go 'off the rails'. It wasn't until a disaster happened that they went to Bill and gave up the horse. Naturally not with the admission that they couldn't cope with it but because the horse was stupid or they didn't find they were getting on with that particular horse any more. And there was Bill with a crazy horse and a hard-done-by officer. Even so he was always very careful never to wade in and take an officer's horse away from him, even when he suspected that things weren't quite right. 'You can tell a policeman he's a bad driver. You can take his wife away from him, but whatever you do don't ever take his horse. Then you'll have an enemy for life.' That was Bill's motto.

It was not until the officer himself no longer wanted to ride his horse that Bill would ask Sara if she could take it on and try to get it back on track. The fact that this upset Ulrich and a few others didn't bother him. As the chief he was responsible for the personnel being used in the best possible way, and he had seen Sara's remarkable ability to get the horses on her side. Nor was she a coward, and it was a matter of showing who was boss, she or the horse. It was both more humane and more economical for him to get Sara to help than to send the horse to the slaughterhouse.

Sometimes it took a long time to get a horse like that back

on track. She had to use all her skill and psychology to reach the horse mentally. But she also had to work physically hard to try and convince a six-hundred kilo police horse, with a will of its own, that it couldn't just do what it wanted. For Sara it was worth all the effort in the world. She could take comfort from the fact that she enabled a number of horses to be kept alive. After a while they would be used for duty again and Bill didn't have to buy so many new horses.

Trying to get disobedient police horses back on duty with a different rider was no new thing. Ulrich and a couple of others had had the job before. But the result hadn't always been so great. The fact that Sara, a young officer and a woman to boot, was succeeding where they had failed, jeopardized Sara's existence all the more. Behind her back things were shaping up for a future disaster.

7

Parade

Parade was a horse nobody wanted. He was really difficult. He preferred to stand on two legs rather than four, and he had never understood that he was expected to behave like a quiet and calm police horse! Ulrich and Vernon, as commanding officers, had told Bill that they didn't want to see that horse on duty ever again. On the latest occasion, in traffic, it had gone quite mad and disappeared at full gallop into a park, its rider powerless on its back. Their definitive view was that slaughter was the only option.

At the next staff meeting Bill brought up the problem and asked whether anyone could consider taking the horse on. Nobody showed any interest so Bill turned to Sara. 'Could you consider having a go?' Sara hesitated; she had seen Parade's 'performances'. This was not a horse to play games with. Ulrich smirked arrogantly. He was sure Sara would never dare mount Parade. The alternative for Parade, a young, healthy and happy but maladjusted horse, was death. Sara could not say no. She had to try.

Sara tackled her task with the greatest care and trained Parade purposefully and patiently. She discovered that the horse was totally confused and terrified of more or less everything. On the other hand he was absolutely convinced that it was he who knew best which way they were supposed to go and not that person sitting on his back. He also thought he should decide their speed! When he didn't get his own way he behaved like a spoilt child. He stamped his feet on the ground, he shook his head and he tried to look as angry as possible.

Sara, who knew that Parade's life hung on her getting him to understand what she wanted, battled desperately to win his trust, but also his respect. He had to learn that he could rely on her in every situation, and that she knew best. It was no easy task to try and reach into the confused horse's soul. Sara was well aware that she had to learn to 'ride' Parade's mind just as much as his physical body. She had to reach him on a spiritual plane in order to have any chance at all of communicating with him. She had to learn to detect his thoughts before he had a chance to convert them into physical action.

In a horse's eyes a boulder behind a bush could very well be a hungry lion just waiting to attack. A little leaf rustling or a squirrel dashing up a tree may be enough to make him turn and run for home and safety. Sara quickly learned to recognize the signs when the fear in the horse was about to gain the upper hand and then to prevent unexpected reactions. She gave Parade the impression that she relied on him completely, but she was always on her guard so that she could forestall him. Bit by bit she taught Parade that he could stand still and look first instead of rushing off the moment he was frightened. She always had plenty of sugar lumps in her pockets. Every time Parade overcame his fears he got a sugar lump. That meant that he increasingly frequently went forward of his own accord to whatever he had been frightened of before, stood still and waited for his sugar lump.

The bond between Sara and Parade grew stronger every day, and at the same time so did Parade's self-confidence. On the rare occasions when he reverted to his old fears, Sara acted very decisively and with great assurance. When she showed him what he had been afraid of, he was always just as much ashamed. He showed it by not even deigning to bestow a glance on the frightening object, but instead just making it seem as if he was completely uninterested. He also began to function more and more on duty and out in traffic. Sometimes Sara was almost moved to tears when she saw how the horse did everything to please her.

Even on her free days Sara went into the police stable to ride Parade. Something very special had grown up between her and the horse and she didn't want to risk any 'relapse'. Naturally she wasn't paid for those hours but that was not something she even thought about—until the day when Ted, the staff representative, called her into a room and asked what she was up to.

'You surely don't think you can come in here and work for nothing? You must realize that that suits our employer down to the ground?' He was bright red in the face with rage. And it didn't improve things when Sara looked uncomprehendingly at him and said that it was more important to her for Parade not to lose his trust in people again than for her to be paid. Didn't it matter how the horses felt as long as the police officers got paid? Of course Sara couldn't hold her tongue but said what she thought before she turned and walked out. Ted was hopping mad. She was absolutely hopeless. How the horses felt? Trust? Didn't care about money? What on earth was the woman talking about?

Sara continued to go to work on her days off. It was enormously irritating of course. People started calling her a blackleg in the corridors.

She and Parade increasingly merged into one. After a while he didn't just work as a police horse, he also began to display a great talent for dressage. She began to train for her trainer,

Dave Anderson, who had helped her with Bobby for many years. She arranged all this training in her free time and she paid for it herself.

Thanks to all the dressage training and the trust which Sara had managed to build up between herself and Parade, he gradually became the safest horse in the Mounted Police.

Now it was Sara and Parade who had to take the lead in difficult situations on duty, when it was a question of getting through at any price. Parade trusted Sara one hundred per cent and she him. She did not realize that this was disastrous as far as some of the male officers were concerned.

Previously the commanding officers had always ridden first. But since their horses had turned back on several occasions and refused to go on, Bill had decided that Parade should go first. Since horses are herd animals it is absolutely crucial whether the first horse goes forward or turns. He's the one who leads the herd and thus also tells the other horses whether there is any danger or not.

Parade was a wonderful horse. It was just as if he understood when it really mattered. Sara could feel how he became absolutely calm and had complete control over himself when he was expected to go forward in front of all the others. He was totally concentrated on Sara and what she wanted him to do. Whenever there was a crush of yelling people thrashing wildly about, with flags and banners, Parade went where Sara asked him to go. On ordinary days he could still sometimes be a real 'mischief' but when things were serious he pulled himself together and didn't try to do his own thing at all.

It was the same when the time came for competitions. As soon as Parade got into the dressage arena he was a miracle of obedience. It was just as if he thought, 'Is everyone looking at me now?' Not to mention how he preened if he got prizes and rosettes. Sara couldn't help but laugh at him, her beloved Parade, who by now was like a part of herself.

She had ensured the support of the police chiefs in her competitions by pointing out to them the value of good PR for the police. She had guaranteed that it would never take precedence over her duties. She would only ever compete in her free time. Nor would it cost the police force anything. With these promises Sara was allowed to have Parade for competitions. At her request she had also been granted permission to hire the police horse-box, which meant that at weekends, together with Bill, she could drive off to competitions with both Parade and her own horse Bobby.

Naturally that was not something that Ulrich could accept. He tried every which way, with Vernon's help, to get a ban on driving civilian horses in the police force's vehicles. In the end he succeeded and Sara was told that the horse-box should not be used any more.

Since Bobby was getting rather old anyway, Sara decided to retire him from competitions. But he was still a healthy and happy horse who knew many of the most difficult movements in dressage. There was no way she could keep him in his stable at the livery where he was. It cost quite a lot every month and it wasn't the right place for a retired horse either. He needed to go out to grass every day and be ridden without any demand for competition performances.

Sara was lucky and managed to sell Bobby to one of the riders in the national dressage team. He liked the horse's abilities and good temper and would use him as a teaching horse for pupils who came to him for training.

Sara was well satisfied. She knew that Bobby would be there as long as he lived. He would be well looked after, go

out in a big field every day and be ridden by talented, ambitious riders.

The competing with Parade continued. Sara had an old horse-
box which she hitched to the car when they had to go anywhere. Since she was working all week, the weekends were
generally free for them to travel. Ulrich was disappointed.
That was not what he had had in mind when he had worked
on the police chiefs.

The persecution of Sara did not diminish. Ulrich did
everything in his power to mould opinion against her and her
competitions. If he had the slightest chance to claim that she
should be on duty over the weekend, he never missed it. Even
if it was obvious that Sara was not expected to work, Ulrich
whipped up such a mood that Bill didn't dare do otherwise
than send her and Parade out.

Each time that happened Sara felt more and more exposed
and alone. If she hadn't been living with Bill, it would have
been easier to point out how unreasonable it was, that she
should first work a 40-hour week and then also be on duty for
some special occasion. But Bill was afraid that he would be
blamed for favouring Sara in some way. The result was that
instead she was 'punished'.

Sara wondered a lot about why Ulrich was so intense in his
crusade against her. Admittedly she had rejected him quite
abruptly that time, several years before, but surely he should
have got over that by now? She just couldn't understand what
was driving him to put all his energy and all his time into
ruining things for her. She also wondered how it was that he
so often managed to get the other officers in their unit to follow his lead. They weren't bad people at all, just indecisive and
easily influenced. But why didn't any of them dare raise any

objection? When any one of them was alone with Sara, they moaned about Ulrich and his eternal harping on about her, at the same time as they encouraged her to stand her ground against him. But when they were together and Ulrich was leading them they were like little lambs who just followed meekly.

When Ulrich failed to stop Sara competing on Parade because she wasn't allowed to use the police box, he was obliged to find some other way. As soon as he and Vernon had the chance, they told other officers who weren't in the Mounted Police how awful it was that Sara was allowed to compete with her dressage horse specially purchased by Bill. She didn't have to work, of course! What's more she couldn't have done even if she had wanted to because her horse Parade was only trained for dressage!

At first Sara couldn't understand why the policemen in the streets looked at her with obvious disgust when she came riding by. One day an officer who was completely unknown to her asked how it was that she was out riding on duty. 'Aren't you out riding for pleasure then? Have you gone the wrong way or...?' Her colleague smiled superciliously when he spoke to her. Sara was both annoyed and surprised at this unexpected attack. She realized more and more how Ulrich was working to undermine her existence as a police officer. The man wouldn't give up. 'But of course that isn't your fine dressage horse which Bill bought at the police force's expense? You can't use him on duty can you? The asphalt would ruin his legs of course?'

There was no mistaking his glee. Sara was so angry she didn't know what to say. Where should she start? She realized that it was an impossible task to get her colleague there and then to believe her and her version. She contented herself with telling him that this was Parade, 'her dressage horse', she was sitting on and which she always rode on duty. He looked a bit crestfallen and muttered something inaudible.

Sara understood that there were a lot of officers who had been led to believe that she was only in the Mounted Police in order to ride for pleasure. She was after all living with the boss so it was obvious that he made sure she didn't need to work! And as if that weren't enough, he had also bought an expensive dressage horse called Parade for her to have for competitions. It was all done in work time and at the expense of the police! Hardly surprising that Ulrich and Vernon, who had told them that, were upset! These rumours were not something that Sara could do anything about. She could only hope that the officers who saw her on duty with Parade were sensible enough to realize that Ulrich and Vernon were not telling the truth. But she felt terribly depressed in the knowledge of the rumours that were spread. She thought a lot about what she should do about it. She didn't expect any help from Bill. His hands were tied and his credibility was so undermined that it was pointless for him to come to Sara's defence.

As so many times before, Sara sat down and wrote. She addressed a letter to one of the senior police superintendents, the chief who was ultimately responsible for the Mounted Police.

'This is an extremely personal letter, written not in anger, but in great sorrow. My role as a police officer and competition rider in dressage is frequently the subject of discussion between one person and another, but seldom in my presence. I feel as if I never get the chance to reply to unjust allegations, so I am writing this letter as one human being to another. I am doing it because I quite honestly feel I am being discriminated against. Please just give me three minutes of your time and hear my appeal to you.'

Sara wrote on, she felt that if only she could talk about what was happening and how she was treated by some of her colleagues, she would get help. She weighed every word. She just had to get the police superintendent to understand that something had to be done to stop the spread of the rumours. She continued:

'If it had been a football team which had won the cup, the ovations would have been thunderous. When I win on a police horse there is a deafening silence and suspicion is cast on me instead. Discrimination—yes, maybe that is a big word, but police dogs compete and that is seen as fine and OK. In other towns my colleagues compete on their police horses and that does not draw any criticism. Why is there so much fuss about me and what I do?'

Sara read through what she had written and went on to report what her working day was like and how the days had been during the years she had been with the Mounted Police. She ended the letter:

'Thank you for being prepared to take the time. I didn't know what else I could do as it has been impossible to speak to anyone who perhaps both would and could do something about my situation. I really don't know how long I can stand this if the rumours are not stopped.'

When Sara sealed the envelope she felt hopeful. She was absolutely convinced that now she would get help and that Ulrich and Vernon would find out that they had to restrain themselves in their witch hunt. The days passed and Sara waited to hear something from 'higher places'. She waited in vain. The letter did not bring about any changes at all. She didn't even get a reply from the police chiefs. She realized that there was no help to be had from anywhere. It should of course have been natural to turn to the union, but for Sara that was not an option with Vernon and Ted as her 'representatives'. To try and bypass them, go direct to the leadership, was inconceivable. If you didn't go via your own representatives, you had no case. Sara felt absolutely powerless.

The riding magazines often wrote about Sara's and Parade's successes in competitions and the fact that the two of them worked in the police force. Ulrich became more and more furious.

When Sara and Parade came home from Germany and the European Championships in dressage for mounted police with a silver medal, his cup was full. After lobbying senior officers for some considerable time, together with Vernon and Ted as the union representatives, he finally achieved a small success. He managed to get a ruling that one shouldn't be allowed to ride one's 'own' horse when off duty.

He had suddenly realized that the police horses were not insured and that this might be a useable argument. Just think if something were to happen when Sara was out riding in civilian events? It was no help to Sara that she could show the police chiefs that she had thought of that. Both she and Parade had been insured for a long time. Ulrich managed to get a ruling passed which banned you from coming to the workplace and riding your horse when you were not on duty. Sara could still travel and compete but not train the horse in her free time.

Now Ulrich made it a systematic arrangement that he would ride Parade himself as soon as Sara was free. Sara was in despair. When she came back to work after her days off, she could hardly recognize her beloved Parade. He was totally hysterical and scarcely fit to ride at all. It took her several days to calm him down and then straight away it was her time off again. The situation was untenable.

In desperation Sara tried to talk to Bill about it, but he couldn't do anything in the situation they were in–that was his defence. He was himself upset about Ulrich's action but he felt quite powerless. If only it hadn't been Sara's duty horse, he would have intervened without hesitation; now he simply didn't dare. However much he loved Sara and suffered when he saw her despair and heard her entreaties that he should intervene, he felt quite unable to do anything. It was a terrible situation which cut him to the quick and made him deeply unhappy.

Sara knew that Ulrich rode Parade for one reason only: to make sure that the horse was in such a state that she could neither work nor compete on him. How could he let a poor innocent horse be caught up in the crossfire just to get at her? She just couldn't understand Ulrich and what it was that motivated him. She didn't know what happened to Parade when she wasn't there. But it was quite obvious that the horse was going out of his mind and that she had to do something.

Day and night Sara thought about what she should do. If Ulrich treated Parade badly to make him unrideable for her and she couldn't stop it, was the only solution for her to give away Parade? Could she do that? Would she be able to put up with not being able to ride her beloved horse any longer and seeing someone else on him? Would Ulrich carry on his campaign in that case? Naturally he wanted to make sure that nobody else would be able to use Parade either. That would only confirm that Sara had trained him correctly.

In the end, when Sara had turned over all the possible and impossible alternatives, she made up her mind. If Parade was

Ulrich's horse, he would be obliged to ride it as well as possible, otherwise he would fail where she had succeeded in having the safest police horse in the stable. If he didn't succeed, he would be thoroughly shamed and lose all his credibility.

When Sara asked Bill what he thought, he looked relieved. 'That's the best thing you could possibly do in this situation.' She knew he was right. However despairing she was, she had to put a stop to the persecution of Parade.

At the next staff meeting Sara put forward her proposal. Since she and Ulrich rode so differently it wasn't fair to Parade for both of them to ride him. She had now decided that since Ulrich was so keen to ride the horse and wouldn't consider stopping, he could have him altogether. There was an awkward silence among the officers at the meeting. Everyone knew what Parade meant to Sara and what work she had put into winning the horse's trust. But nobody said a word. Nobody opened their mouth and said what they thought. They didn't dare. Rose was naturally incredibly upset but she was quickly silenced. All the other big strong policemen sat like frightened kids and looked around furtively.

Sara knew that many of them were shocked by Ulrich's attempts intentionally to ruin Parade's mental health, but she also knew that when the chips were down they would not dare to oppose him. After what seemed an eternity, Bill broke the silence. 'Well that's great. That's that sorted. From now on Parade is your duty horse, Ulrich.'

The atmosphere was tense. Sara held her breath, what would Ulrich say? Finally he opened his mouth. 'I certainly don't want that damned horse, it's crazy!' Bill didn't hesitate to reply, 'But then you won't want to ride him at all if he's that crazy, will you?' Ulrich was bright red in the face and beside himself with rage. 'Of course I don't want to!'

Sara couldn't believe her ears: Ulrich wouldn't ride Parade any more and she could keep him? But it was really true and that night Sara slept better than she had for a very long time.

8

Accidents?

Even if Parade was no longer openly the subject of persecution, the situation still just got worse. Strange and frightening things began to occur. Every time Sara was due to go off and compete with Parade, something happened that meant that she couldn't go.

The first time this occurred was when she had her car and horse-box parked outside the police stable all day, so that she could drive off with Parade to a competition directly after finishing work. When she was due to start, the car wouldn't go. A little earlier she had driven it into the yard and thought then that the engine sounded a bit strange. Now it was absolutely impossible to start. Instead of going to the competition she had to be towed to a garage.

When she fetched the car a day or two later, she was met by a puzzled mechanic: 'Why on earth do you have sugar in the petrol tank?' 'Sugar?' Sara wondered what he meant. But yes, the fuel filter had been completely blocked with sticky caster sugar. 'I think I'd get a lock for the petrol tank cap if I were you,' said the mechanic.

On the next occasion it was time to compete, Sara was met in the yard by the grooms when she came to fetch Parade. One of the girls came towards her: 'You won't be able to ride that horse for a good while; he's got an abscess on his back which is so tender you can hardly touch him.' Sara went in to see Parade. Quite true; just where the saddle should sit there was an abscess, almost the size of a cherry. It was hurting so much that the horse almost lay down when Sara touched it. She took a strong lamp and shone it on the horse's back to try and see what could have caused the nasty abscess. She squeezed it carefully and a little puss came out. She talked soothingly to Parade, who was looking extremely unhappy. When she squeezed one more time a little steel pin came out. Sara looked carefully at it and saw that it was probably the very tip of a sewing needle. How in the world had it got there? Poor Parade. There was nothing she could do to cure his ills and naturally there was no question of any competition.

After about a week without riding him, the abscess had gone and Sara could ride Parade again as usual.

After a while it was time for another competition. But when the same thing happened again Sara realized that Parade was in real trouble. If they couldn't stop her any other way there was evidently someone or some people who were prepared to use any methods whatsoever. She shivered when she thought about what they might be prepared to do with her beloved horse if they were desperate enough to want to stop her for good. Was it worth it? Could she risk Parade being injured several times just because she wanted to compete on him? The answer was obvious: of course not. Would she have to stop competing? Was there no way to put a stop to this madness?

Apart from the letter Sara had sent to the police chiefs, she and Rose had tried speaking to them in person on several occasions. After all, now there were two of them who could attest how Ulrich and his henchmen were behaving to make life as wretched as possible for them. Naturally Sara was not able to voice any suspicion that Parade was being sabotaged and deliberately injured, but at least she could tell them how the injuries always coincided with the competitions. Each time it had seemed as if these mighty gentlemen had listened attentively and even thought of doing something about the situation. 'This is really intolerable,' was a phrase used frequently, which Rose and Sara soon learned meant: this is something we can't do anything about. It was precisely as if they thought that if only the girls had the opportunity to get it off their chests everything would be fine. The result of their requests for help was that Ulrich and Vernon were promoted. Sara talked to Bill about her fears for Parade and that something even worse would happen if nobody put a stop to it all. He was absolutely horrified at the idea that Sara might voice her suspicions to anybody. 'You can never prove anything, so whatever you do, don't say anything.' Bill was more worried about Sara not being able to hold her tongue than about the fact that there were police officers in his department who were evidently prepared to sink to any depths to stop her competing with Parade.

Sara thought over what she could do. She felt that she needed to get away for a while. Away from the Mounted Police but also away from Bill. They had lived so much on top of one another, both at work and at home, for three years, that it wouldn't hurt them to be apart for a while and distance themselves a bit from the problems. But she couldn't leave Parade for any length of time so she had to try and get him with her. She could go to her trainer, Dave, who lived a few hours drive away. He had often suggested to her that she could come and stay for a while to train and help him with his horses. Martin had his school, so he couldn't come with her, but he would be fine with her mother and Erwin.

Sara admired Dave and liked him a lot. He was very skilled and had ridden both in the Olympics and in the World Championships. But that was not all; Dave was a person with 'an old soul'. With him she could talk and he always listened. It didn't matter whether they talked about horses and riding or about deeper subjects. Their discussions were always just as rewarding.

Bill thought it was a good idea for Sara to get away for a while and for her to take Parade with her. He signed her application to the superintendents for time off with Parade. A few weeks later Sara got the go-ahead. Now she could start to plan her trip. Naturally she was worried that someone or something might stop her plans. But she comforted herself with the thought that the person or people who wanted to put a spoke in her wheel would surely be glad that she was going to be away for a while.

Everything seemed to be OK when the day for her departure arrived. Sara put Parade in the box and drove off. It was a winter's evening and it got dark early. When she was halfway there she discovered that the engine was worryingly hot. She stopped at the side of the road. When she opened the bonnet water was spurting out all over the place! Even with her small understanding of engines and their hoses, Sara realized that she couldn't drive another yard. Alone with a horse in the box in the dark, on the motorway with about a hundred miles to go in either direction, she knew that she was really in dire straits. She didn't have a mobile phone either. She had to get help somehow. Nobody seemed to notice her need for help when she signalled wildly at the cars speeding by. Finally she realized that she would have to leave Parade and walk off to ring for help.

She went to the nearest house, directly opposite across a field. It was pitch dark and she couldn't see where she was putting her feet. She tried to cross a ditch and prepared to jump. But she didn't see the barbed wire lying on the ground and caught her foot at the same time as she jumped. She fell headlong on the bank and lay still. A terrible burning pain in her left arm caused her to cry out loud. She was almost fainting. Finally she managed to get up and stagger on to the house on unsteady legs, and she rang the bell. She fell unconscious into the arms of the astonished woman who opened the door.

It was now many, many years since Sara had had any dreams about her previous existence. As the years had passed her memories had also receded. She had almost forgotten how terrifying they had been. But now she drifted into 'the dream' again. She was back in the same abyss once more. All the horrors rose to the surface of her consciousness again.

She sees her mother and father, whom she recognizes so well, and other people sitting around them. They are all sitting as still as mice; their fear is so manifest that you can almost touch it. She hears the tramp of boots and doors being slammed. Men's voices are shouting and she huddles up in her father's lap. She is weeping silently. She knows that the least rustle will mean death and she is shaking all over. She is once again a child seeking comfort and security in her father's arms.

'Wake up' the nurse shook her hard. 'You must wake up now.' The nurse slapped her firmly on the cheeks and slowly Sara returned to reality. Still with that fear in her body and not quite sure where she was, she opened her eyes.

'Hello, now you really are awake!' The nurse looked kindly at her. 'Where am I?' Sara was in total shock through what she had experienced in her other consciousness. She had almost managed to repress that terrible existence and now it was back. She could remember everything with crystal clarity.

The nurse told her that she had been anaesthetized for a

while because her arm was quite badly injured. Her elbow had been dislocated and both the ligaments and the joint capsule were torn. It had all been repaired but her arm was in plaster and would have to stay like that for a while. Parade was in the stable of the woman where Sara had rung the bell, and the car was already in a garage.

Fortunately the kind lady who had opened the door had realized that something had happened to Sara's car. Her husband had gone to investigate and found Parade patiently waiting in the horse-box. So instead of time off and training with Parade, it was sick notes and a return home.

When Sara fetched her car from the garage a while later, history repeated itself. It was a very concerned mechanic who came to talk to her: 'Either you have unusually unpleasant acquaintances or you have rats in your car who eat hoses.' He held up a piece of hose to show her. 'It looks as though it's been cut a little bit and then the pressure of the water has done the rest.' She looked at the hose and saw that the man was absolutely right. What's more, it wasn't just one hose that had been demolished; all the hoses looked the same.

Sara shivered, she knew it wasn't rats, of course...

9

'Ready-trained' police horses— and Mozart

When Bill heard what had happened, he didn't react at all as Sara had expected. Instead of being worried about her and confirming that it couldn't be a coincidence that all the hoses had been broken, he assured her time after time that she shouldn't talk to anyone about the fact that she thought the car had been tampered with. 'Whatever you do, say nothing. There will be a terrible row if you so much as breathe a word about it. That's precisely what they're waiting for. You can never prove anything, you know that.'

He insisted and Sara was obliged to promise him not to talk to a single person, not even Rose. It was of course impossible to conceal that the accident had happened, but Sara had to pretend that the car had broken down for no reason.

She took Bill's inability to act to mean that he didn't want to help her and that he was too much of a coward to deal with the situation. She couldn't understand him at all. She didn't see how Bill was suffering and how depressed he was. She just felt alone and abandoned. Emotionally they were not communicating and they were losing touch more and more. They took all their misery home with them at the end of a day's work, and their conversations, which had once been so intimate, were increasingly replaced by fierce arguments.

Bill really loved Sara with all his heart, she knew that, but she also knew how torn he felt between his love for her on the one hand and his anxiety to be a fair and good boss on the other. Sometimes she felt that he had treated her unfairly and unnecessarily harshly in his position as boss, particularly when he really wanted to show that she didn't enjoy any privileges whatsoever. Not even the privileges which other people in the department had. Sara had learnt to live with it, but now something else had crept into their relationship. Bill's anxiety about people suspecting him of not being up to his job had made him blind and deaf to Sara's fear and to her need for help. Help which she would undoubtedly have received, and had the right to receive, if only they had not been a couple.

Finally Sara suggested that they should separate. Bill seemed almost relieved. He agreed with her that it was an untenable situation and that neither of them could carry on with things as they were. But they would always have a very special affection for each other, which nobody could touch. No conflict could destroy their spiritual relationship.

During the time when Sara was on sick leave, Rose rode Parade. Sometimes Sara drove to the police stables to pay a visit and watch her riding. One day when Sara was standing watching Rose and Parade, Vernon Stone came along. 'What are you doing here, you're supposed to be off sick?' He was red in the face and his voice was angry. Sara explained that it was not much fun to be on sick leave for so long and that she just liked to pop in because she didn't have much else to do. Normally when colleagues visited their workplace they were welcomed with coffee and biscuits, but she, Sara, was not allowed to put in an appearance at all.

'I didn't know there was any ban on popping in when you're on sick leave. Does it only apply to me or ...?' Sara couldn't conceal how angry and upset she was by his attack. 'If you

show yourself here again I'll report you to the benefit office.'
Vernon lifted a warning finger. 'What's more you can jolly well
go home and dig your damned great garden instead.' He
didn't for a moment try and conceal how he disliked her and
how her house stuck in his jealous throat. Sara turned and
went before he could have the satisfaction of seeing the tears
in her eyes.

After her long sick leave Sara was back at the Mounted Police.
She had decided to stop competing with Parade. She didn't
want to risk any more accidents. She and Rose continued their
work of breaking in and training the young horses which were
bought. Over the years they had become more and more
united, not least after all the attacks they had had to weather
together.

One day a majority of the staff told Bill that they wanted a
new instructor. It was the commanding officers who were
supposed to give instruction but after many and long discussions the staff had come to the conclusion that this didn't work
very well. Now they put forward a request to have Sara as their
instructor instead. Bill was naturally surprised but nonetheless pleased. At least there was some hope, he thought to
himself when the request was put forward. He promised that
he would think about it and see what he could do. Sara was
naturally pleased at their faith in her; perhaps finally she could
be one of the group?

Ulrich was absolutely furious when he heard what the staff
had done. Not content with declaring him unsuitable, what is
more they had put Sara forward. He immediately began to
work systematically on as many of them as he could. 'This is of
course a way for Bill to give Sara authority and get her into the
boss's seat, can't you see that?' He agitated and carried on until

in the end Bill had his back to the wall. Now the staff wanted to know what he thought of the idea of making Sara the instructor.

'But it was a request which came from you, are you mad?' Bill was almost angry that the staff should question his motives. Ulrich was not slow to take up the argument: 'You must surely see that nobody meant that she should have the title of instructor and what's more an instructor's salary. It's us, the commanding officers, who get that.' Once more all the officers at the meeting sat there as quietly as shamefaced children and looked down at the floor. The meeting ended with everything being left as it was. To Ulrich's great delight.

But he was very annoyed that the horses trained by Sara and Rose worked so well on duty and were often praised by his colleagues. He decided to do what he could to change that state of affairs. He thought about it for a long time and finally he knew what he had to do: he sat down and wrote a rationalization proposal to his superiors. He wrote and told them how much Sara and Rose cost the police force every day and how expensive it was to train young horses. 'Instead we should buy in ready-trained police horses' he wrote, and he went on: 'Horses like that can be bought anywhere and in the long term they will be much cheaper, even if they're more expensive to buy initially. This way we can get the two officers who spend their time training young horses out on duty instead.' Ulrich was really pleased with himself when he read through what he had written.

When Bill saw Ulrich's proposal, he tried to explain to the chiefs that it was not quite as simple as Ulrich let it appear. For one thing there were no 'ready-trained' police horses for sale, they had to be trained for what they were going to be used for. For another thing Rose and Sara were the two most efficient officers he had; they rode twice as many horses, twice as well and for just as long as the other officers. What is more he could still use them when he needed to for special assignments. But his words fell on deaf ears. Ulrich had prepared the ground well. He had known that Bill would object. 'Bill is backing Sara up so that she won't need to work as a police officer. Even if they're not living together any more, Sara has power over him.' Ulrich had been very careful to explain in detail how Bill would try to protect Sara.

Bill was told that the proposal was worth trying and Ulrich received a large sum of money for his initiative. Many years later it would become clear that this was an expensive mistake for the Mounted Police.

But not everything was misery for Sara. One day a man rang the Mounted Police and asked to speak to her. He told her that he had set up a kind of foundation to provide promising and skilled dressage riders with the possibility of buying horses which were particularly gifted in dressage. Since he had understood that Sara was no longer competing with Parade and that Bobby was retired, he thought she should go and look for a fine horse and tell him when she had found one.

Sara couldn't believe her ears. Was she to have the chance to buy a selected horse and be one of the few people to be part of this project? 'If you have managed to reach high dressage with two horses, of which one also had to work as a police horse, it must be a good thing for you to get a horse which is actually meant for dressage, surely.' The man was very kind. Sara learned that she only had to pay one third herself and the foundation would pay the rest. With the agreement that she would immediately begin looking for a suitable horse, the conversation was closed.

She immediately began to enquire. After searching for a while she found him. Mozart was jet black and powerful. But he moved easily and rhythmically. She felt, when she tried him out, that he was strong but not precisely trained in dressage. But she knew straight away that she and Mozart belonged together! She loved him from the first moment and she was convinced that he would prove to have an aptitude for the difficult art of dressage if only he were trained.

If Sara was overjoyed, there were others who ground their teeth. But no one and nothing could dampen her unqualified joy at having the chance to buy a horse such as she could only have dreamt of.

After a week or two, when the vet had examined and approved Mozart, Sara went to fetch him. In a happy mood she drove off in her car with the horse-box hitched behind. There were a few hours' drive ahead of her so she put her foot down and drove almost too fast. She had the radio on. But then she began to hear a strange noise. 'Knock, knock, knock,' the sound was getting louder. She switched off the radio to hear what it was that was making the noise. It was getting louder all the time. Fortunately she was able to turn off into a petrol station and stop. When she got out of the car and looked it over she could see immediately what had caused the knocking. She caught her breath when she saw how one wheel on the horse-box was almost falling off! The wheel was held on by just one nut. The other nuts had come off.

Sara asked the man at the petrol station to come and see if he could help her in any way. The helpful man took the horse-box into his workshop and put it on the ramp; Sara went in with him to see. 'Well you've been really lucky, if you'd had a horse in there both you and the horse would have flown off the road.' He pointed to the threads on the wheel nuts which were all, apart from one, completely shorn off. 'I've never seen anything like it, how in the world did that happen?' The man was talking to himself as he examined the wheel housing.

Sara was absolutely shattered. She knew that it was no coincidence. But were there no limits to what they would do? Just imagine if she'd had Mozart in the trailer? Sara discovered that she was shaking all over and the kind man smiled sympathetically. 'I can understand that you're frightened just thinking about what might have happened, but luckily there's no major damage. The problem is just that you can't continue towing the box, you'll have to leave it here. I'll arrange for it to be repaired and ring you when it's ready.' Sara thanked him for all his kindness and together they managed to uncouple the trailer. There was nothing for it but to phone Mozart's owner and tell him that unfortunately she would have to fetch him at a later date.

A few weeks later she went back to the petrol station where she had left the trailer. It was repaired now. When she paid she saw that the man was looking worried. As if he wanted to say something but didn't really know how. Sara helped him get started: 'Could you tell whether the nuts were so worn that they fell off?' He seemed relieved that she asked. 'Admittedly it's an old horse-box, but the likelihood of four wheel nuts shearing off at the same time is not exactly great . . .' When Sara looked enquiringly at him, he continued: 'If I didn't know better I would say that they'd been sawn off.' He looked almost horrified by his own statement. 'Sawn off?' Sara shivered, she realized that the forces working against her were prepared to go a long way, cost what it might. Shaken but relieved that the horse-box was OK again, she drove to fetch her new horse.

Mozart, to whom Sara had given the forenames Wolfgang Amadeus, was stabled at the riding club which was quite close to the Mounted Police stables. When she started spending more time in the stables where she had Amadeus, as she normally called her horse, she noticed that a few people there were somewhat aversely inclined towards her. Not many, but a few.

The police had a time for training every day in the riding school which belonged to the local club. Sara's riding of sometimes ungovernable police horses had been watched with great interest. Not least because Ulrich had been only too happy to point out how bad it looked. Some people had the impression that Sara's horses were always unruly and that it was just her fault. Nobody had tried to find out why she so often rode these difficult police horses. Ulrich was never slow to confirm that of course it was Sara who caused the problem. The fact that they were horses which neither Ulrich nor any of the other officers wanted or dared to ride was something he didn't mention. The fact that Parade was used as a lead horse was not noticed either. But when the horses reared up on their hind legs and tried to throw her, that was noticed with great interest. Not because they were afraid that Sara might be injured. It was the poor unfortunate horse they were worried about.

'Look, surely she's pulling too hard!' 'No, now she's hit him with her stick!' 'Poor horse!' These comments were frequent and encouraged the whole time by Sara's colleagues in the Mounted Police. Naturally Sara knew how they carried on, but she also knew that they were speaking from their own ignorance and ill-will. For her it was more important to save a horse's life than try to accommodate different points of view. She knew that whatever she did it would be the subject of discussion, so there was no point in even trying. It was almost a little ironic that they should question her handling of the horses, when it was precisely her love of these animals which led her to take them on time and again and try to sort out the ones which had 'gone off the rails'.

Sara wondered a lot about why she always 'managed' to become the subject of people's pronouncements. For some reason it seemed as if everybody 'knew' what she was doing and everybody had a view on it. They 'knew' what she was thinking and even had views on that! Sometimes complete strangers would come forward and start talking to her. In a way it was nice but when they too 'knew' everything about her, she was sometimes rather appalled. She had done this or that, or else she had intended to do it and that was just as bad! The fact that Sara herself had no idea what they were talking about didn't matter at all, they 'knew' of course! She couldn't understand how people had the energy to get so involved. Surely there were better and more important things to devote themselves to?

Amadeus shaped up well and after a while Sara was able to begin competing with him. Having been spoilt with Parade, who had loved showing off, Sara now learned that Amadeus was not always in the mood! Sometimes he was more off the ground than on it, even in the dressage ring. He couldn't always control his energy, but most of the time Sara managed to keep him on track and then they were among the best ranked.

This was not something that was ever talked about openly at Sara's workplace. It was as if the civilian competition world didn't exist. If Sara had a competition planned for a weekend when she was off duty, Ulrich or Vernon did what they could to make sure that she was 'needed' on duty. So every time Sara was supposed to go off and compete she was very careful not to let anyone know about it as far as possible. That was an effective way of preventing sudden requirements for extra personnel and for avoiding the risk of her car or trailer being suddenly unusable.

10

The chief's job?

When Ulrich's proposal had been fully implemented and there were four 'ready-trained' police horses in the stable, bought by Vernon and Ulrich, Bill thought that it would be bound to end in disaster. So when he was suddenly offered his retirement, he accepted.

That was the worst thing that could have happened for Sara. Now anybody could apply for the chief's job and she knew that there was an imminent risk that Vernon or Ulrich would get it. So she decided to apply for the job herself. The police chiefs had let it be known that it would be a good thing if the applicant were a woman, since there were no female officers in equivalent grades. Sara thought it might be worth trying. She had been a police officer for sixteen years and worked in the Mounted Police for thirteen, so she must have enough experience, she thought. She submitted her application forms hopefully. After a while she was invited to an interview. Sara was very surprised when she understood that Vernon would be present. She was given no explanation as to why.

There was then a very unpleasant interrogation in which Sara was forced to answer quite honestly about how she viewed the situation in the Mounted Police and why she felt motivated to apply for the job. Vernon sat silent for the most part, but now and again a scornful smile escaped him, when Sara reported how she viewed the situation. There was also another union representative present, monitoring the interview. But he was more inclined to adopt Vernon's scorn than take Sara's word for things and see the seriousness of her allegations. When the interview was over and Sara left the room, the others stayed behind. She could hear them laughing behind the closed doors.

Weeks went by and finally Sara was asked to see one of the police chiefs' representatives, who was also the person who had conducted the interview. He welcomed her and opened the conversation: 'Well you wouldn't have done a bad job as head of the Mounted Police unit, I'm sure of that. But,' he continued, 'history is of course against you.'

'History?' Sara looked at him enquiringly. He hastened to add, 'Well you know you are a controversial person who people like to talk about a lot.' He looked hurt as Sara continued to look uncomprehendingly at him. 'So do you mean that just because there are people who gossip about me, I can't be the chief?' She was trying to speak as calmly as she could, although she almost jumped up in her anger. 'No, no, I didn't mean it like that, but you do put a lot of people's backs up, you must realize that at any rate? You have a certain habit of saying what you think and that's not always a good thing, if I can put it like that...'

Sara was speechless and he continued: 'I mean it's not such a good thing that you can speak up for yourself and formulate your ideas in writing. Not to mention how it annoys a lot of people that you are such a good rider. It's really your own fault to some extent ... You could try and conceal your talents a little more so that then people might be able to get on with you as a person. Quite simply you rub too many people up the wrong way, that's the sum of it.' Sara didn't know what to say. She was absolutely stunned by this back-handed 'praise'.

Finally she found her voice again: 'Do you mean that I am

being blamed for being able to speak, write and ride well? I thought it might be an advantage if a boss in the Mounted Police had those qualifications?' She bit her tongue when she saw how he drew himself up and adopted a determined expression. 'Well now you will have to step back this time and show that you can work together with Vernon and Ulrich. They have complained about their problems in working with you several times and it's a serious matter. You must face the future with confidence and try to fit in, then perhaps you'll have your chance later on.'

'If Ulrich or Vernon becomes the boss at the Mounted Police I will have no future there, can't you understand that?' Sara looked at the man sitting in front of her. He had taken the complaints Ulrich and Vernon had lodged against her seriously but he had never bothered about what she and Rose had reported when they had tried to get help. Suddenly she realized that all that talk about equality and the desire to see women as bosses was perhaps just playing to the gallery? It sounded good that the police were really working for equality between the sexes but when it came to real life the women were 'steamrollered'. The men stuck together and appointed each other. If a woman should manage to get in, she had to be good but absolutely not too good because then she would be far too great a threat. On the other hand if she was merely 'good' there were plenty of male officers who were really good! Why should they appoint a woman then? That argument had obviously won so far and perhaps there was no reason to change it?

Sara, whose anger slowly changed to despair and resignation, felt the tears beginning to sting the backs of her eyes. She cursed herself and her own lack of self-control. But her inability to get the man in front of her to understand what she had had to put up with over the years and the fact that instead he put the whole blame on her, was just too much for her. He looked at her almost sympathetically, 'Well now, is it really as bad as all that? Surely not.'

Sara tried to pull herself together so that she could continue talking without crying. 'If Vernon and Ulrich are allowed to run the Mounted Police the way they want, it won't be many years before the police don't have a Mounted Police unit any longer. The "ready-trained" police horses don't really work out; only on paper, according to Ulrich. The staff will transfer to other departments since it's really Ulrich and Vernon who have problems working with other people. Not to mention what it will be like for the poor horses.' Sara didn't measure her words. She no longer cared what the police super-intendent thought; she had to get it off her chest. 'I really don't think it will be as bad as you say, at least let's hope not,' he asserted in a fatherly, somewhat protective tone of voice. Sara could not in her wildest dreams imagine that he would ever have talked to a male officer like that.

When she left the room she was devastated. Not just because she had been treated in a humiliating and unfair way, but also because it had been made so obvious that all those fine words about a woman officer having the same rights as a man and positions being filled entirely on the basis of com-petence and suitability were just so much hot air! She thought back to the day many years before when she had been inter-viewed for admission to the police training college. How uneasy the man who had interviewed her had been that she might one day feel like writing about the police force and what it was really like. She had not understood his concern at all then; now it was suddenly easy to understand.

She, Sara, was naturally not the only woman who had been

treated like this when an appointment was to be made. It surely couldn't be a coincidence that there wasn't a single female officer in the uniformed service. In the CID it was not at all unusual to find women in senior positions, but in the regular police force they were conspicuous by their absence. One might ask why? Were all the women police in the uniformed service really so incompetent that they couldn't compete with the men?

Sara didn't know the answer to this question but she found it hard to believe that this really was the case. She only knew that she had qualifications which were worth far more than Vernon's or Ulrich's but 'she had to fit in and show her good will'! Was it really acceptable to be treated like that? She felt her adrenalin rising and she was glad she had left the room. She was no less angry when she thought back to what it had been like in the Mounted Police when Vernon had been standing in for Bill as the boss.

On one occasion one of the horses had gone lame. It had begun in a fairly low key way but both Sara and Rose had pointed it out time after time to Vernon. In the end the rest of the staff had also noticed it but the horse still had to be on duty, by Vernon's express order: 'We haven't got that many horses we can use, so he'll have to get walking,' had been his response. Finally the poor horse had been standing on three legs and was completely unable to put any weight on the fourth. Vernon had not even considered calling the vet, but given the horse painkillers himself and hoped that it would get better.

In the end, after several days when the horse had lain down and refused to get up, and the staff were in uproar, he had allowed it to be transported to the animal hospital where the horse could be X-rayed. The vet had been shocked: the horse's sinews and ligaments had completely collapsed in the bad leg and mercy killing had been the only humane solution. But what had Vernon done? Taken the horse home again and left it lying there for another week before he could finally decide that it really would have to be slaughtered in any case.

On several occasions the staff had openly and loudly talked about cruelty to animals. In the end Vernon had realized that it was actually best to do something. Sara felt she wanted to be sick when she thought that he might be the next boss of the Mounted Police.

Bill left his job and it became official who was to succeed him: Vernon. The news reached Sara, through some of her colleagues, that Vernon had already been appointed to the job at the time of her so-called interview. It became clear to her that the interview had simply been a ploy. Of course they had been obliged to interview her, for the sake of appearances, but the position was filled even before they did. Sara was appalled at their cheek. And as if that weren't enough, Vernon had even been there and marked her for the job she was applying for, in his capacity as the union representative! He had even sat and boasted to some of his colleagues how he had marked her down in order to eliminate the risk that she might really have a chance of becoming the boss.

'Just imagine what the protests would have been like if ordinary people knew how things are done.' He had been very detailed in his description of how easy it had been to eliminate Sara's chances. Even if the people listening thought this was too bad, there was nobody who dared to say anything. Vernon was their new boss.

His first action as the boss was to give Ulrich the job of working in the daytime with the training of horses and riders. But since that meant a lower salary, he made sure that Ulrich got remuneration for that. Sara and Rose, who had been trying for years to get some remuneration for the same thing, had been silenced and criticized. And yet it said in Ulrich's job description, and had done for many years, that he should be responsible for training. His wage and title were based on that.

But in actual fact it was Sara and Rose who did the job, without either the title or the extra remuneration. Now Ulrich was even going to get an extra allowance! Sara and Rose couldn't believe it was true! The only answer they had received when they had tried had been that they could always talk to Bill, he was surely their 'staff representative'. They had also written to the police chiefs on the subject but never received any reply.

Sara soon realized that Vernon had decided that her days at the Mounted Police were numbered. 'There'll be two of us to see who has to hang up their boots first, you or me!' He didn't even try to conceal his dislike of her when he had one of his first talks with Sara after his appointment. Rose, who was present and heard what he said, was shocked by his open 'threat'. 'He can't do this, he will make your life hell just to get you to leave. What are we going to do?' Sara felt Rose's anxiety and despair and she really didn't know what she should do. Even then she still didn't know just what Vernon and Ulrich were capable of.

Parade was now entirely in their hands. Now they were getting their own back for all the years of bitterness and rage at Sara's and her horse's successes.

Parade was getting on a bit and for several years he had had one of the four loose boxes there were in the police stables. The other horses were tied up in stalls. Parade had also been tied up until Sara had managed to change things, with the help of the vet. Parade was an escape artist; he had learnt how easy it was to get his head collar off at night. After he had got out a number of times, the grooms had been obliged to tighten the collar so much that he was almost suffocated, just to stop him getting out. Sara had not been able to bear it, but had asked the vet if it was really all right for a horse to be kept in such a tight head collar. The vet had immediately assured her that Parade should be loose in a box with a door instead, which is what he now was.

Vernon changed this straight away. He put Parade into the smallest and darkest stall of all and tied him up as tightly as necessary with a head collar so that he couldn't get out. In desperation Sara felt how tightly he was tied. She couldn't even get her fingers in between his neck and the strap, and she couldn't hold back her tears. She fell nervelessly on Parade's neck and poured out all her despair. What should she do? Parade looked at her with his big dark eyes and pushed at her with his nose. It was as if he was trying to say, 'Get me out of here, I can't stand it here. I am relying on you to help me.'

Never before had Sara felt so totally helpless and powerless. She couldn't do a thing to help her beloved horse. She was forced to accept the boss's decision that Parade had to stay where he was. Nor was she allowed to have a blanket on him like he was used to since Sara had taken him on. There was always a draught, both from the outer doors and from the hay-loft, which was why Sara had always covered Parade over during the coldest part of the year. 'Surely you know that a police horse doesn't feel the cold? Do you want to put a blanket on him when he has to stand still down in town on duty in 25 degrees below?'

Vernon shouted and yelled at her. Sara couldn't believe that a grown police officer, who was moreover appointed superintendent, could allow himself to lose his cool so completely. It was no better when Sara pointed out that the risk of that was not very great since no police officer sat still very long on his horse at 25 degrees below freezing either. Naturally no argument was accepted. If the horse was cold he would have to put up with it.

Of course Parade was also systematically taken out on all conceivable and inconceivable duties. Not with Sara in the saddle, no, with different riders every time to really show her that now her 'monopoly' on the horse was well and truly over.

Sara saw how Parade was slowly but surely broken down, mentally as well as physically. From being a proud horse with incredibly great self-confidence and a glint in his eye, the horse that now met her was one with a defeated look and resignation. From having had a muscular body and glossy coat, Parade now stood with his head hanging. His coat was shaggy and his muscles had disappeared. Sara could not believe that it was the same horse who had previously greeted her so cheerfully with his welcoming neigh every morning. When Parade didn't even lift his head when she called him, she thought her heart would break.

She pondered a great deal on this barefaced wickedness. What was it that drove these people so far in their hatred that they exposed an innocent animal to such treatment just because they wanted to hurt her? It was basically her fault that Parade was suffering. If she had not been so stubborn but had backed off, perhaps they would have been kinder to the horse. Sara suffered the torments of hell, not least when she blamed herself for what was happening. Why had she not just fitted in? Why did she have to stand up and protest every time when she thought something was wrong? Why could she never hold her tongue?

Now it was too late; there was nothing she could do to help Parade. Her entreaties would only lead to the view that she had finally been beaten and that would make things even worse, Sara was sure of that.

Finally she decided that she had to leave the Mounted Police. Even if that was a victory for Ulrich and Vernon, she couldn't stay any longer. She couldn't stand seeing Parade and not being able to do anything.

She now made one last attempt to talk to the same police superintendent as before. She wanted to explain her attitude and tell him why it was impossible for her to stay. Once again she sat in the chair facing his desk. She related as calmly as she could what things had been like lately. She told him about Parade and what he had to put up with, but also how she was being treated. She reported a conversation she had heard between Vernon and a colleague.

The colleague had ridden Parade and pointed out to Vernon that there was something wrong with the horse's legs. He had thought that it was noticeably lame in one foreleg. Vernon had admitted that he knew that, but said that since the 'ready-trained' police horses were still not fit for duty, he was obliged to use Parade. He would make sure the horse got so many painkillers that nothing would show. 'He will have to serve on all the special assignments over the summer and then we can have him put down in the autumn.'

When Sara repeated this conversation the superintendent looked a little shocked, but that was as far as it went. Sara realized that no action would be taken against either Ulrich or Vernon. She asked herself how it was possible that it seemed to be accepted within the police force that both people and animals could be persecuted? Sara asked to have a year out from work. Even though it felt as though she was abandoning both Rose and Parade, it was impossible for her to stay at the Mounted Police unit.

She had tried being an 'ordinary' police officer for several years before and that was not something she wanted to go back to. Admittedly the spirit of fellowship and the working environment had been completely different from the Mounted Police but the work itself was so draining that Sara felt she couldn't bear it. She admired the officers who managed to keep going year after year. She couldn't understand how they coped with dealing with all the misery they encountered. Nor was there any option for her to apply to any other department. Somehow it felt as if the police force was now a closed chapter. But she was too unsure to hand in her notice, so she took up her right to take leave of absence instead.

Sara had also begun to wonder whether she was right to accept the way she had been treated when she applied for the chief's position. Surely it was not possible that for instance the Equal Opportunities Ombudsman would look the other way if it came to his notice? She knew that she was qualified enough. The problem was that she was a woman and not a male police officer.

11

A new reality

Sara left the police to try and earn her living by teaching other riders privately and helping them to train their horses. She knew that there was a great need for that. She had had to say No many, many times over the years when riders had asked her for help.

Sara was glad to get away from the Mounted Police for more than one reason. To her despair she had seen how the years there had changed her. And it was not for the better. She discovered that it had become hard for her to trust people. She found it difficult to see the good in them. It was almost hard for her to believe that people even wanted to be good.

She, who previously had always been an open and positive person, had become more and more reserved in her contacts with other people over the years. She who always, no matter how dark things had seemed, had been able to see the bright side of her existence and the good in people, now saw things from a different perspective. Slowly and imperceptibly the years in the Mounted Police had changed her into a suspicious and cautious person. It was only now that Sara realized how they had managed to change her whole personality into one that was actually alien to her.

In all the years with the Mounted Police Sara had written almost nothing. It was as if her inspiration had been blown away with the wind. Now she felt a need to express herself in writing again, and it was her anguish which came out:

From deep inside my depths
there comes a cry
a cry of anguish
life, life, give me
just a second
of life
a second of clarity
a second of light
a second of the stars'
distant light
give a hint of a
heavenly light
give to the darkness
in my soul
a little hopeful ray of sun,
give to my body's hidden soul
hope of eternal life,
give to the earth's darkness
a hint of an eternity.

A lot had happened in the Mounted Police over the years which she would never get over: what they had done to her beloved Parade and how they had driven her to doubt people's goodness were a part of it.

Certain incidents in her work had also marked her soul deeply. There were various incidents but the one she remembered most of all and which she never ever wanted to experience again, was when she as a mounted police officer had been obliged to protect neo-nazis shouting slogans and waving flags and banners with the red-white-black symbol which stood for death and destruction. Sara remembered every minute of the terrible scene which she had been obliged to take part in. She remembered her shock at having to witness how it was once again possible for the odious swastika to wave in the wind, while battle songs thundered from the loud-speakers. She had heard those choruses before; she remembered them well from her childhood nightmares.

She had sat there in uniform on her horse, without any possibility of getting away from it. Terrifying images had chased one another before her eyes and surrounded her in all their evil. With her colleagues on horseback she had been ordered to protect these nazis. Their opponents had gathered in huge crowds and both sides had equipped themselves with various kinds of weapons. The mounted police had been lined up between them. Sara had managed to get a grip on herself after a while, until she encountered a pair of eyes which were so filled with hate that Sara recoiled. The face of a young woman, crazy with anger, had etched itself in her memory for ever.

From the woman's mouth hurled the words: 'Nazi whore, nazi whore.' At that moment the world vanished for Sara. An icy hand gripped her heart and twisted it. When she heard the words 'Nazi whore' echo in the infernal cacophony around her, it felt as if everything turned upside down. Through the noise she had heard the words which were thrown straight in her face. Everything spun round for her and she lost her balance.

Later she would always remember with gratitude how Parade had helped her. When he had felt how she fell to one side of him, he had quickly parried and moved in under her. Sara had recovered her balance and managed to stay on the horse. Thanks to Parade she had not fallen off, to a probable death in the hate-filled and crazed mob. Later she would remember how she had reacted, how important it had been for her not to allow those repulsive words to melt into the lava flow of hatred which was encircling her.

She had opened the visor on her helmet, her face was as if carved in white marble and her eyes black with rage. When she called the young woman over to her, the reply was, 'What do you want, you Nazi hag?' The woman came up to Sara and her horse with a threatening mien. Sara bent down for the woman to hear what she said: 'You have no idea what you are saying when you accuse me of being one of them.' Sara pointed with her stick to the roaring herd of wild animals who called themselves neo-nazis. 'If you could only imagine for one second how I feel having to stand here and protect them. I could have been one of you, but this is my job which I have to do, whether I want to or not. I tell you my whole soul is in turmoil.'

The hatred in the woman's eyes vanished and they were filled instead with wonder. For a fraction of a second their eyes met in mutual understanding and then the woman turned. She was obviously one of the leaders of the anti-racists gathered there: 'Leave her alone, she's not one of them. She's a real human being!'

When Sara pulled down the visor over her face again it was to hide the tears streaming down her cheeks. None of her colleagues had noticed the drama which had been played out and which—for good or ill—had etched itself in her memory for ever. She knew that she would never again be able to bring herself to take on a similar assignment.

Rose was broken-hearted at Sara's decision to leave the Mounted Police—and her. She had no possibility of doing the same herself and was simply obliged to stay put. She didn't have any particular desire to drive around in a radio car in some suburb or sit in a criminal department and investigate crime. The alternative was to grit her teeth and stay. Sara consoled her with the thought that it might just be better when she was not there. Then nobody would need to carry on and bully Rose for working with her, Sara. They would see each other every day, since the Mounted Police stables were so close to the riding club.

At the end of the summer Rose was able to tell Sara that Parade had also left the Mounted Police now. Vernon had done precisely what Sara had heard that he would do: Parade had had to work the whole summer and had received painkillers. When the autumn came he had been taken to the slaughterhouse. In normal cases when a horse was to be put down, it was not driven off to the slaughter-house, since horses have amazing premonitions and an ability to smell blood and death. Therefore during his time as chief Bill had introduced the rule that all horses should be put down in the yard so that they should never have to experience the fear of death. But Parade had been driven to the slaughterhouse.

Sara's despair and total powerlessness in the face of this absolute evil really opened her eyes. She was almost afraid of herself when she felt the intensity of the hatred which welled up inside her. It crawled through her body like an enormous worm. She wanted to shake it off, but she couldn't. Her whole soul knew that the hatred inside her was detrimental and destructive. In her despair she prayed to the good forces which she knew were there somewhere inside her that she might be able to forgive. She remembered the meeting she had had on the beach as a child; the strength which she had received from Him. She couldn't allow herself to feel such a deep and devastating hatred towards another human being as she felt now. She had to listen to the Voice inside her, which she knew would always help her if she asked for it.

12

Preparations

Sara now moved her work to the riding club, where she had Mozart. She soon had plenty to do. She had several horses to ride full-time and a lot of riders came to her for private lessons with their horses. She was glad she seemed to have full working days and spent all her time at the riding club. Every day she was filled with an indescribable feeling of happiness. She felt as if she had been born again. She could breathe again and laugh and be happy. Only now did she realize how close she had been to being spiritually suffocated. She was wholly happy for the first time in many years.

Mozart was everything she had dreamed of, and more besides. Sara felt privileged to be his rider. Together they trained to achieve the best possible results.

Training a horse in advanced dressage can be compared with training an elite athlete, at the same time as learning to play the most sensitive of instruments. The harmony between the horse and the rider is the decisive factor in success in dressage. It takes several years of patient training to get a horse to carry out the most difficult dressage movements with ease. The horse had to be trained both physically and mentally in order to have the strength. Getting Mozart to dance under her, getting him to carry out the most difficult movements in perfect harmony with her, gave Sara experiences which she had only dreamt of.

More and more pupils streamed in every day and before

Sara knew where she was, she had so much to do that she had to refuse various offers of clinics they wanted her to run. She also received an enquiry from a riding journal as to whether she would consider regularly answering readers' questions about horses, traffic and the law. With her experience of police work and horses in traffic she was tailor-made for the job, the editor thought. Sara was delighted to accept.

The days at the riding club passed quickly. Sara worked from early morning to late at night. She felt as if she were floating on a cloud. Even though she was working far longer hours every day than she had with the police, it was worth anything on earth to be able to put that behind her. She pushed away the thought that she was only on leave and that one day she might have to go back. She was convinced that everything would work out for the best if only she had faith and relied on its sorting itself out.

She faced the future with confidence. It wasn't just the teaching and the riding which provided her with an income; her column in the riding journal had developed and become very popular. Sara felt encouraged by all the response she got and thought it was fun to write again. Even though it placed quite different demands on her from any she had faced before, it was a challenge to answer every question as well as possible.

Since Sara now spent so much time at the riding club, she began to notice things which she hadn't thought about previously. Every day, for instance, strange cars came and took feed from the feed shed. At first she didn't think too much about it, but when the traffic continued day after day she began to wonder. She thought it was best to ask the newly appointed head of the riding club, Cyle Connor, what was going on. That proved to be a mistake. Sara was totally disconcerted by his unexpected reaction. 'That's none of your business. And if you don't take care I'll make sure you have to get out of the club.' He wagged a finger in her face and looked extremely threatening. Sara recoiled without saying a word. His outburst was totally unexpected. Sara felt her heart pounding with the shock. She really didn't understand anything. But when a little later she needed to ask him for a sum of money, which was supposed to be set aside for dressage riding, and he couldn't tell her where it was, she began to suspect that all was not well. Finally she felt obliged to contact the board of the riding club which was ultimately responsible for everything which went on in the club.

If she had been surprised at Cyle's behaviour, it was nothing compared with the way she was received in her meeting with the board. Their opinion of her was quite decided, as they immediately gave her to understand. They knew that she had been obliged to stop working as a police officer because she had difficulties in working with her colleagues and because she was so unkind to the horses. They had actually received all the necessary information about her from the commanding officer at the Mounted Police unit and there was no point in her trying to tell any stories!

Sara almost fainted when she heard them. At first she could hardly find the words, but she managed to say that she had not left but simply taken leave of absence. What was more she had never been unkind to any horse! She was speaking to deaf ears. They had clearly decided 'what sort of person she was'. Indeed they knew, and she should take care otherwise perhaps she wouldn't be wanted at the club any more. On top of that, to come in and insinuate that the riding school boss had something to hide was so ridiculous that it beggared belief. She was not to come and try and stir things up like she had in the police.

Sara left the room. She felt as if she had had a bucket of ice-cold water poured over her. How was it possible to spread such lies about her? How could she stop it? She realized with horror that the only possibility was to counter-attack. The Equal Opportunities Ombudsman! She would have to write to him and appeal against the chief's appointment. That was her only chance to put a stop to it, she realized now.

But she made the mistake of telling her decision to a few friends. Or more correctly, people she thought were her friends. It didn't take long before Sara's plans became known in the Mounted Police. If she managed to get a hearing for her application to the Ombudsman that was the worst thing that could happen to Ulrich and Vernon. Sara had to be stopped.

During this time Cyle Connor, the head of the riding club, had taken on a private secretary, Veronica List. Her official title was club secretary, but Sara could not forbear from wondering how she had come to be appointed. With an astronomical salary as well! Veronica had nothing to recommend her for the job she was supposed to do, but perhaps she had other qualifications which Cyle appreciated?

Now Cyle and Veronica together took over the whole riding club. The riding instructors rallied behind them after negotiating the highest conceivable salaries and other benefits which Cyle had enticed them with. The board sat back and relaxed; they had every confidence in their riding club manager. Large sums of money were turned over every day and major transactions were done. Everything went through Veronica's hands without any controls whatsoever. It was to transpire later that she was an unusually devious woman.

Sara saw how the 'deliveries' of feed continued, and also a steady stream of teaching horses were replaced and slaughtered. Veronica sat like the spider in the web. Cyle made sure that nobody questioned anything. The employees received anything which took their fancy and Sara, who seemed to be the only one with suspicions, was silenced. And considering how she had been received, perhaps she should not get involved if assets disappeared from the club.

Sara was unhappy about the situation. So when the annual accounts were made available prior to the AGM of the club, she sat down and went through them carefully. The auditors had signed to say that everything was in order, but Sara was horrified when she saw the figures. What did an auditor know about how much feed over a hundred horses would eat in a year? Not much, Sara decided. Nor had the auditors reacted to the fact that twenty-seven teaching horses had been put down in one year, which was naturally horrendous. Those horses had been insured and the insurance money had also been paid out, but 'disappeared' along the way. Nor was the number of riding lessons correct. Sara saw that about half were 'spirited away'. Not even the absence of the sponsor money, which seemed to have been swallowed up into the ground, was noticed by the auditors. When Sara had finished she realized that there were very large amounts which had disappeared from the club's finances.

What should she do? She was absolutely certain that Cyle and Veronica were not to be trifled with, but she could not stand by and watch them stripping the club of money. After some mature consideration, Sara decided to make another attempt to talk to the board. Surely they must realize what had happened if she went through the figures with them. She was wrong. She was not even allowed to have her say before they showed her the door. How did she have the nerve to come to them and call the club's employees into question? They were

Barbro Karlén,
2 years old

Barbro Karlén,
2½ years old

Barbro Karlén,
7 years old

Barbro Karlén,
12 years old

Barbro Karlén
EN STUND I
BLOMRIKE

I
Barbro Karlén
BEGYN
NEL
SEN
SKA
PADE
GUD

Wezäta Förlag

Barbro Karlén

DET KOM
FRÅN ETT
BARN

Barbro
Karlén

Lärarinnans
brev

WEZÄTA FÖRLAG

Some original Swedish editions of Barbro Karlén's books

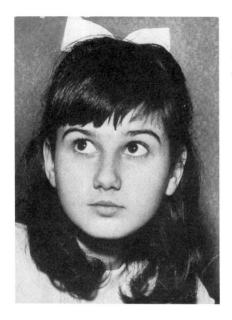

*Barbro Karlén,
about 12 years old*

*Barbro Karlén,
18 years old*

In the police force, 1981

Barbro Karlén (right) with a colleague, 1989

Taking part in a police dressage competition, late 1980s

Photo: Tomasz Tarczynski

In the Mounted Police, around 1989

On the cover of the magazine:

Svenska JOURNALEN

Nr 16 2 augusti 1991
Årgång 67 Pris 14:50

*Från skrivande
underbarn till
ridande polis*

**Barbro Karlén
om
framgången,
hästarna
och livet**

Sydafrikansk
kyrkoledare:
Vår uppgift
är att medla

*Grillfest i
trädgården*

Vallonerna –
invandrarna som
byggde
Sveriges välstånd

481—16

POLIS

Photo: Erik Lindahl

On the cover of Svenska Journalen, *August 1991*

*Barbro Karlén,
1997*

Photo: Patrick Elias

*Barbro Karlén,
1998*

people they themselves had appointed and whom they knew were both competent and honest. Was there no limit to her meddling? What the police had told them about her was obviously true!

The unsuccessful attempt to get the board to open their eyes resulted in Cyle getting even worse. The harassment really gathered momentum now. Sara was happily unaware that because of her insistence she had set herself up for a disaster.

One night there was a break-in at the club office, where all the accounts were kept. Somebody had tried to set fire to the computer, but failed, as luck would have it, not least considering that over one hundred horses could have been burnt in their stalls. That had obviously not bothered the perpetrator who clearly was not an expert on arson. The fire brigade established that somebody had poured white spirit over the computer, presumably in the belief that it was flammable. The result was thick black smoke but no real fire and the computer was still useable. Even then not a single person reacted and the incident was soon forgotten.

But Cyle and Veronica were worried at Sara's interest in the finances. And as if that were not enough, it looked as though she had managed to involve some elements of the dressage section, which had also begun to ask awkward questions. It would be disastrous for them if someone took Sara at her word and carried out a proper audit; they were agreed on that.

What should they do? They consulted each other and discussed it back and forth and eventually came to the conclusion that they would have to frighten Sara so much that she would shut up. Perhaps a threatening letter would have the desired effect? 'Get out of the stables before something happens to you.' Not particularly intelligently formulated, but they decided that it would have to do for the moment. Veronica stuck the flap down and put it in the letter-box when she and Cyle drove home.

But the letter didn't have the desired effect. Sara realized that she really was on the trail of something that someone wanted to hide at all costs. Now her curiosity and anger were seriously aroused. A lot of other people would perhaps have chosen to give up and keep quiet but not Sara. She always wanted to get involved even if it meant disagreeable consequences. It seemed she would never learn. . .

Cyle and Veronica began to make plans for their next step. Sara had to be got rid of as quickly as possible. In no circumstances should she appear trustworthy and it was essential to act quickly.

One day when Sara was riding Mozart in one of the three maneges in the indoor school, she heard the teaching horses on the other side of the wall being skittish and running around. Riders were obviously being thrown off too, because she heard someone cry out. It did sometimes happen that the teaching horses put a little colour into their otherwise drab existence. They would become like frisky colts and if one of them started to have some fun the others would also seize the opportunity to follow suit.

Mozart also got a bit excited when he heard how they were galloping round and kicking the walls. But Sara soon calmed him down and continued to ride. She was on her own in her manege. There was a plastic curtain between the maneges so that you couldn't see what was happening on the other side. Suddenly one of the riding instructors, Ken Lehmann, came rushing in to her: 'You really must stopping whipping your horse, can't you hear how the teaching horses are getting frightened out of their wits?' He was yelling as loud as he could. Sara stopped and asked him what he meant. 'Didn't you hear me, stop ill-treating your horse, people are getting thrown off because of you!'

Sara sat on Mozart in a puzzled state as Ken turned and left. What on earth did the guy mean? Sara wondered if he was out of his mind. He had admittedly never been particularly nice to her, nor to anyone else for that matter, but even so he really had gone too far now. She heard Ken on the other side of the hanging: 'Yes of course, it was Sara who was the cause of your horses getting frightened, but now I've told her she's got to stop whipping her horse.' She couldn't believe her ears. She couldn't just let him stand there unopposed, so she rode after him into the other manege. He came towards her with a crop poised in his hand: 'If you don't ride out of here then I'll help you.' Sara realized that there was absolutely no point in talking to him, so she left the indoor school with her horse. She wondered why in the world Ken had reacted so oddly. She thought that he must have had a really bad day and vented his feelings on her.

But it was to emerge that this behaviour was not an isolated incident. It became systematic. As soon as Sara was riding on her own in the school and a lesson was going on in one of the other maneges, she was accused of being the cause if the teaching horses became frightened of anything. On every such occasion Ken or one of the other instructors charged in to her and yelled as loudly as they could that she should stop whipping her horse. Naturally the riding pupils got the impression that it really was Sara's fault if anything happened.

After a while Sara was told that the board wanted to talk to her. They had received complaints about her riding and now people were demanding that Sara should leave the club. The board pointed out that they were well aware how she had treated the poor police horses over the years. Ulrich and

Vernon had been completely beside themselves when they had informed the board about her carryings-on in the Mounted Police. She needn't think that she could come here and carry on with the same things she had been dismissed from the police for!

Helplessly Sara tried to tell them the whole story. But she realized herself how hopeless it was. Where should she start? The members of the board were looking at her with disgust and suspicion. They closed the meeting by telling her that she should really watch out in the future; they had their eye on her. Cyle and Veronica were keeping them informed of her behaviour.

Sara felt as if she were caught in a glass cage, whichever way she turned she came up against a wall. Any attempt to fight the powers she had against her was doomed to failure. But she was, as we have said, stubborn, and sometimes also extremely foolhardy. She considered various options. Reporting suspected misappropriation of funds was one alternative, but she soon ruled that out. She knew what it took to get an enquiry set up; she knew that it wouldn't be easy to convince the police when not even the board was prepared to see what was going on.

Finally she pulled herself together and contacted a newly appointed member of the board, Jim Pearson. Sara hoped that he was not yet too 'indoctrinated' about her person but that she would really be able to talk to him. Jim listened to her attentively, in spite of the fact that he 'knew' all about her. He didn't say much but made little notes while Sara talked. She told him of her suspicions and how she had been treated by Cyle and the riding instructors after they had learned that she was questioning the accounts and the finances.

She told him how lately people seemed to systematically

accuse her of causing accidents in the indoor school through her riding, and that she was absolutely convinced that it was one line of attack in the attempt to get her out of the club. She also told him of her thoughts of writing to the Equal Opportunities Ombudsman about the chief's appointment in the Mounted Police. She explained how some of her colleagues had made life hard for her and how their spreading of rumours over several years had actually ruined her chances of promotion.

After their conversation Sara heard nothing for a long time. She assumed that Jim was just as indifferent to finding out anything awkward as the rest of the board. But suddenly Cyle was sacked. Sara learned that a massive audit had been carried out and that they had found hundreds of thousands of crowns missing on the accounts. The board hadn't just sacked Cyle, they had also reported him to the police. Then they put the lid on it. No further information was forthcoming from the board.

Sara discovered to her horror that now they had put Veronica in sole charge of the money and the business. When Veronica had realized that the audit was an unavoidable fact and that she and Cyle would be uncovered, she had switched sides. She had been most helpful and heart-broken when she realized how Cyle had tried to cheat the club of money! She helped the board in every way to sort out all the strange transactions. That way she had also managed to conceal her cooperation with Cyle. Without hesitation she had left him to the mercy of the board, which had finally woken up.

It didn't help when Cyle tried to tell them that he was innocent and that it was Veronica who was the brains behind all the transactions. Veronica, overwrought and weeping, had complained to the board how Cyle had even managed to pull the wool over her eyes. The blue-eyed board gratefully accepted her offer to take care of the finances and the day-to-day expenses for the time being.

So there was no great change in spite of everything. Instead of Cyle and Veronica draining the club of money together, she did it on her own. She was far more adept than Cyle had been and now she had a little more scope for action. Nobody knew that Veronica was well experienced in this field. Her speciality was draining the money from companies and then disappearing. Her previous 'subject' was several millions the poorer. Both of her parents helped her with the business, but behind the scenes. So far things had gone well for the family; there were already several millions on foreign bank accounts and more was to follow. The only cause for concern at the moment was Sara.

Veronica thought back over the rewarding conversations she had had with two of the police officers in the Mounted Police. Hadn't one of them been called Ulrich? He and his colleague had let it be understood that they were not a bit keen on having Sara back in the police force. They were also terrified that she might appeal to the Ombudsman about an appointment, for which she felt she had been discriminated against.

Veronica realized that they had a shared interest. One of the police officers had even said that he was prepared to assist her if in some way they could help each other to get Sara out of the way. Veronica pondered over how best to exploit the situation. Getting mixed up with the Mounted Police, in spite of the fact that she had been on the wanted list for several years, was not something that bothered her. She understood that the mounted section was not so much in touch with reality to keep an eye on who was on the wanted list.

So Veronica, Ulrich and Vernon put their clever heads together. After some brain-storming they knew what they had to do. They would make sure that Sara was once and for all driven out of the ring, both in the police and in the club. They would apply the principle that if a lie is repeated enough times, it comes to seem like the truth. All the rumours which were already circulating about Sara would be exploited. Ulrich promised to use a contact he had. Veronica and the instructors would take care of the rest. The game could begin.

The riding school instructors now became even more frenzied in their attacks on Sara. As soon as someone fell off they rushed in to where Sara usually rode and called out 'Sara, now you've got to stop whipping your horse, people are falling off!' This sometimes happened by mistake even when she wasn't there, but the riding school pupils who were on the other side of the screen didn't find out. The private riders who happened to be in the manege on such occasions wondered whether the instructor in question was quite right in the head! But nobody said anything. It was too stupid to be worth commenting on, they thought.

Veronica added her mite. She made sure she sat in the café with a view over the maneges, with various other people, when Sara was riding. Time and again she commented on Sara's riding. 'Look what she's doing. Oh didn't you see that? She pulled the horse's mouth as hard as she could and hit him with her long stick at the same time.'

Nobody thought about the fact that it was only Veronica who 'saw'. In the end everybody thought they had seen Sara hitting her horse, and the rumour began to spread.

13

Rumours

Ulrich was very happy with the reports he got from Veronica. Everything was going according to plan. Now it was time to get help from an important and powerful friend he had known for some time. They had hit it off from the first time they met and they felt they had a lot in common.

Sara continued her teaching and riding, quite unsuspecting. She could not in her wildest dreams have suspected what was going on. The noose was being drawn inexorably round her neck but she was still totally unaware of it.

One day when Sara was to take a lesson with one of her pupils, Joo Bergman, she nonetheless got a foretaste of what lay ahead. Joo was upset: 'Sara this is getting really nasty. Do you know what people are saying about you?' Sara looked uncomprehendingly at her. 'They are saying that you don't hit the horses in the indoor school so much because you know that they can see you. But that you go out riding in the forest and have a helper with you who wipes away the bloodstains.'

Sara couldn't utter a word. She looked at Joo, who looked desperately unhappy at having to tell Sara this. Sara asked her to repeat what she had just said, she couldn't have heard right. No, that was exactly what Joo had heard. She assured her that she hadn't misunderstood anything.

'Hit the horses? Bloodstains? Helper?' What was all this? How could such crazy rumours arise? Much less circulate and take root? Sara was absolutely heartbroken but also frightened out of her wits. What was happening?

The fact that Veronica was playing a large part in spreading the rumours became clear to Sara a few days later. Sara was training with Mozart and her trainer Dave, in the indoor school, and Veronica sat as usual in her place in the café, next to the window, together with some other people. She didn't stop pointing out how Sara was tormenting her horse during the training. 'Look now the poor horse has got to step sideways as well!' 'Oh, shame, look how sweaty he is.' 'Look, she's holding him back and pushing him forward at the same time, shame, it's pure cruelty to animals.'

Veronica was agitated. She didn't see that there was somebody sitting a little way behind who could hear everything she was saying. Mary Krause was listening astounded at Veronica's allegations, at the same time as she observed Sara and her horse. Mary, who was very familiar with horse sports in general and dressage in particular, became more and more upset as she heard Veronica's overwrought voice. The training which was going on down there in the manege was exemplary, which did not surprise Mary at all. She knew that Dave was a highly thought of and skilled instructor and that Sara was a competent and experienced rider. Sara was doing nothing wrong whatsoever, as far as Mary could judge. On the contrary she thought the whole thing looked both harmonious and professional.

'Holding the horse back and pushing it forward?' Mary looked out at the manege where Mozart was just demonstrating a wonderful piaff. It was quite obvious that if you wanted to get a horse to trot on the spot, you had to hold it in at the same time as you pushed it forward.

Mary was convinced that Veronica knew that just as well as

anyone else did, so why was she carrying on and talking like she was? The fact that there had frequently been a lot of talk lately about Sara, in negative terms, was something Mary had noticed, even though she didn't go to the riding club very often. She had heard the most improbable rumours from one person and another, but she hadn't taken them very seriously. She had after all known Sara for many years and knew that it was impossible that the rumours could be true. Mary herself had asked Sara for help with her horse a few months earlier. It had begun to be difficult and reluctant, but Sara had solved the problem in a few sessions. Mary had never seen her use any hard methods, on the contrary, she seemed to manage to get the horse on her side in a remarkable way. Since then Mary had had no problems with her horse.

The more Mary listened to Veronica, the more hot under the collar she became. This was no normal 'gossip', this was something much more serious: propaganda which involuntarily led Mary's thoughts back to her history books at school.

'This must be just like it was when people persecuted the Jews,' thought Mary to herself, and she felt herself shiver at the thought. 'This is just what it must have been like, people talk and allege things until other people believe it, even if nobody has seen it for themselves.' She didn't know why she began to think of the Nazis' persecution of the Jews, but she felt that she knew what was happening and she got more and more worked up.

When Sara had finished her lesson and came out to the stables with her horse, Mary went to meet her. 'I don't know if I'm doing the right thing telling you this, but you need to know what is going on.' Mary repeated word for word to Sara what she had heard and what a horrible feeling she had had. When

Sara had heard enough, she asked Mary whether she would be prepared to go with her and speak to Veronica. This time she was going to sort out what was going on.

When they reached Veronica's office, Sara asked Mary to wait outside. She didn't close the door when she went in; she wanted Mary to hear the conversation. 'What is your reason for broadcasting your views on me and my riding?' Sara took Veronica by surprise and she sat up, looking absolutely uncomprehending. 'Me! Am I supposed to have views on your riding?' Veronica looked dumbfounded. 'You know I could never do that, because you are so good and I am only a riding school rider. How can you say such a thing, that's terrible!' Veronica almost managed to squeeze out a tear and look really upset by this terrible accusation.

Mary couldn't contain herself any longer. She had stood outside the door and listened to Veronica's act. Now she couldn't stand it any more. 'Don't sit there and lie through your teeth. I heard every word you said about Sara and her way of training her horse. Cruelty to animals! What are you actually trying to do?' Mary was so angry she was bright red in the face. Suddenly, Veronica changed her strategy. The tears which had begun trickling down her cheeks disappeared and instead her face was distorted with anger. 'What are you doing in here? Get out of my room!' Veronica lost control for a moment when she realized that she had been caught out. 'In any case it wasn't me that was talking about Sara, it was someone else.' She tried to look convincing but failed utterly.

In the meantime one of the members of the board had come into the room and wondered what the raised voices were about. Sara described the situation to him briefly. He looked annoyed but promised to investigate the matter in more detail and see what he could do, but said it was best they left Veronica's room immediately.

The next day Sara got a letter from Veronica. She apologized for what had happened and for the fact that she had spoken ill of Sara. She assured her that it had never happened before. In actual fact it was always she, Veronica, who took Sara's side whenever she heard malicious gossip. Finally she had to say that she thought Sara was always pleasant and kind to her and that was why she was determined to apologize.

When Sara folded the letter up she didn't know whether to laugh or cry. How could anyone be so false? How could anyone bring themselves to behave like that? Sara was quite mystified. She almost felt sorry for Veronica. She kept the letter with its empty phrases. It was obvious that Veronica had been told to write it and that it wasn't even worth the paper it was written on. Nvertheless, it might be a good idea to keep the letter.

A few days later she received another letter, this time without a signature. '*Get out of the stables otherwise your horse will go lame. If you show this to anyone watch out for your hide.*' Again!

Sara thought things were beginning to get really nasty. She thought about taking the letter to the police and reporting the threat. But she soon thought otherwise when she realized that if this got out it too would undoubtedly also be used against her. 'Have you heard about Sara, she treats her horse so badly that she's even had threatening letters.' Instead she contacted the board and asked what they thought she should do. Naturally they had no answer. She hadn't expected one either.

At the AGM the whole board resigned, one of the main reasons being the club's financial situation. When a completely new board had taken office, Sara decided to try again. She had to draw their attention to Veronica and the fact that she had taken up where Cyle left off. It was also a good opportunity for her to talk to them about the rumours which were circulating.

'We have received information about you from the outgoing board.' The woman who sat facing Sara was the new chairman. 'But,' she continued, 'we haven't seen anything ourselves, so we can only judge by what we hear from the employees. They actually come and complain about you pretty often.'

Sara felt overwhelmed with helplessness. Here she was sitting with people who had no idea what was actually going on, and what a can of worms they had opened up. She tried to explain but she noticed that what she said was making no impression at all on the assembled board. Either they couldn't understand or they didn't want to. Neither her remarks about Veronica, nor the fact that it was she, Sara, who had drawn attention to the financial irregularities, nor her attempts to rectify the terrible rumours which were being spread about her could change anything.

In desperation she tried to explain that there was widespread ignorance among the riding pupils, which Veronica and the riding instructors were exploiting in order to make her appear the cause of everything which happened. All in order to drive her out, because she interfered in things which she evidently shouldn't. Sara also told them briefly about her experiences in the Mounted Police. Finally she realized that her words were falling on deaf ears, when one of the members of the board stared at her fixedly and said, 'Well, you'll just have to be careful when you're riding, so that people can't misinterpret what you're doing, won't you?'

'Be careful?' Sara felt her stomach churn at this unfair treatment. She who loved horses and rode them with the greatest of care and precision. She invested all her skill in riding each horse as well as possible and so far she had not failed with any of them. Instead she had saved the lives of a number of horses over the years, precisely because she was able to get them to understand what was right and what was wrong. She had helped a lot of horse owners who had believed that their horses were beyond hope and had become more or less dangerous to ride because they had been handled wrongly.

These people sitting in front of her barely knew which end of a horse was which and here she was trying to explain to them that she wasn't cruel to horses and didn't treat them badly. And they were telling her to 'Be careful'. What's more it was she who had protested about the manager's shady activities and now she was trying to make them understand that Veronica was in the throes of filling her own bank account at the club's expense. And yet somehow it was she, Sara, who was the villain of the piece. When she left the meeting she was convinced that everything was completely mad.

She was happily unaware of what was to come and what preparations had been made. She was also unaware of the eyes which watched every step she took or rode.

On one occasion there was the owner of a stallion who needed Sara's help. The stallion had been ridden for a long time but he had just got worse and worse. Now his owner was worried that he might have to be put down since he was beginning to be dangerous. Naturally Sara was not pleased to be asked whether she wanted to ride the horse, but she didn't want to feel responsible for his not being allowed to live any longer.

So she equipped herself with her riding hat, a stick and an extra rein, all to prevent the stallion rearing up on its hind legs with her, as far as possible. But on the first day that was almost all he did the whole time anyway. When he reared up with her on two legs, without the least desire to listen to her, she hit him with her stick. When the horse then went down on all four legs again, she patted him and gave him a sugar lump. After a while she only had to hold the stick up for him to see when he was thinking of trying to throw her off.

A horse which rears like this one was doing could be absolutely lethal. If a horse loses its balance in that situation and falls on its back, the rider could end up underneath and be crushed to death. Sara was well aware of the risks, not least because it had happened to a woman mounted police officer in Norway just a month or so earlier. She had died of internal injuries.

So Sara knew that it was necessary to get the horse to understand that it was unacceptable to rear up. What's more the reason he did it was because he didn't want to go forward unless he was allowed to decide how and where himself. In order to break the pattern Sara was obliged to get him to respect her and also to show the horse what she wanted him to do instead. The next day, when Sara rode the stallion again, he was considerably more cooperative. After a few more weeks he was not a problem at all. The horse had settled down and the owner was satisfied. Sara could only hope that the two would now work well together. She promised to take time out now and again to help them.

Naturally this incident did not pass Sara's detractors by unnoticed. The idea that one punished a horse who was trying to take his rider's life was suddenly not self-evident at all. How could Sara behave like that to the poor horse? The fact that she gave him sugar when he was good and did what she wanted was also turned against her: 'Look how frightened she is! Now she's even trying to bribe him with sugar!'

14

The nightmare begins

It was Easter and the annual horse show in the biggest indoor arena in town was due to open. This particular year Sara was especially looking forward to the event because Lou Fleming, one of Sweden's most eminent dressage riders, had asked to borrow Mozart for a performance.

Sara had trained with Lou occasionally and Lou had also ridden Mozart a few times too. This time Lou thought it would be simpler if she borrowed him rather than hauling one of her own horses more than 250 miles. After all, Mozart was virtually already there and Sara was happy to lend him to Lou. Basically she was more than a little flattered that it was her horse Lou had asked to borrow. And as if that were not enough, Lou was also going to hold a seminar at the horse show, to demonstrate how she gave training and instruction. And Sara was to ride Mozart to illustrate the instruction. So it was little wonder that Sara was looking forward to the Easter weekend in happy expectation.

Mozart was on his best form. He was alert and happy and Sara trained him carefully. She wanted him to be as well prepared as possible before the performances.

A couple of days before the event, when she was riding in the indoor school as usual, first her pupil Joo's horse and then Mozart, she saw a well-known riding journalist in the café, from one of the biggest daily newspapers in Sweden.

When Sara had finished her turn, she was delighted with

the fact that both Joo's horse and Mozart had had one of their best days. Joo's horse was not so highly trained in dressage yet, but was looking very promising and Mozart had really developed his ability to carry out the most difficult movements. He had managed piaff and passage, pirouettes and flying changes in series without any major problem. Sara felt that it was almost as if he felt the watchful eyes observing their training round.

The day before the Great Day Sara groomed and brushed Mozart very carefully. He was to be absolutely as handsome as possible. She saddled and bandaged him to ride a short turn. Today she was only going to ride for a little while so that the horse would be as fresh as possible the next day.

Just when she was going to take Mozart into the indoor school, she got a message that Eve Pester, the journalist from the previous day, had tried to phone her. She had asked for Sara to ring her back as soon as possible, so Sara put Mozart back in his box again and went to the phone.

On her way to the phone she wondered what Pester might want. It must surely be connected to her visit the previous day? 'Perhaps she has heard that Lou is going to ride my horse at the Horse Show and wants to write about it?' Sara knew that Pester was one of Lou's great admirers. She felt happy and expectant as she dialled the number to the newspaper, even though she was still a little surprised at the interest Pester was showing. Sara knew that Pester wasn't particularly popular in riding circles, since she always had a tendency to write negative articles about horse sports.

'Hello, it's Sara Carpenter, you had asked me to ring?' Sara's tone was good-humoured.

'Yes, it's a good thing you rang. I just wanted to tell you that

I'm planning to write about you in tomorrow's paper.' Eve Pester's tone was not particularly friendly and she actually sounded rather curt. Still Sara replied happily that that sounded nice. 'Are you going to write about dressage in general or about me and my horse?'

The answer she received opened the door to a nightmare. 'It's not nice at all. I'm going to make sure I put an end to you and your riding once and for all.' Pester almost hissed the words. Sara was silent for a long moment before she was able to ask what Pester meant. The journalist continued in the same hissing tone: 'Don't play the innocent. I have heard a lot about you over the years, not least from the Mounted Police. I know what you're up to.'

Sara felt an icy coldness spreading through her body, but she tried to keep cool. She asked what it was that Pester had heard and from whom? 'That's none of your business. But there are some brave people at the club where you ride and they are prepared to stand up and tell what they have seen. And . . .' she continued without even taking a breath–'I saw for myself with my own eyes how you carried on when you were riding yesterday!'

'Yesterday?' Sara couldn't understand a thing. Yesterday was the day she had been so pleased that Pester had seen how well the horses were doing. 'But the horses did brilliantly yesterday, what on earth are you talking about?' Now Sara was beginning to get angry.

'Yes I have to admit it was one of your better days, but I know all about how you ride when nobody can see you. I've heard how you ride out in the forest with your horse after a competition for instance . . .!' Pester sounded triumphant, as if she had really discovered something to prove that Sara was cruel to her horse.

'Yes and ...?' Sara was absolutely puzzled.

'People know what you get up to in the forest ...' Her tone was still triumphant and almost delighting in Sara's discomfiture. Sara wondered how it was possible for anyone to report what happened when 'nobody saw it'? She added that she thought it was nicer after a competition to go for a little walk in the forest than calm the horse down by walking backwards and forwards on the asphalt outside the stable.

'Nicer', snorted Pester, 'anybody can tell what you're doing to your horse when you are alone with it out in the forest.' Before Sara could reply Pester brought the conversation to a close: 'I don't want to talk to you any more, you're just trying to put me off the scent with your lies. I'll be writing about you whatever you say.'

While Sara had been talking to Pester, Steve Meyer, who also rode dressage at the club, had come into the room. He too had evidently been asked to ring Pester, because he signalled to Sara that he wanted to take the receiver when she had finished. Sara, who realized that it didn't make any difference what she said to the journalist on the other end of the line, thankfully handed over the receiver to Steve. She shook her head and was totally despondent.

What was going on? Pester had decided to put an end to her and her riding once and for all? What on earth did she mean? How could a journalist express herself like that? Sara's head was spinning. She sat down on a chair in the room and heard from Steve's replies that Pester was evidently giving her opinions about his riding too. 'Yes, I have to admit that I was a bit hard on him but the horse was being lazy,' Steve tried to excuse himself.

Sara didn't want to hear any more and went out to the stable where Mozart was waiting. Her legs were shaking and she could hardly hold back the tears. She would really rather have gone straight home but she had to let Mozart get a bit of exercise. She decided just to walk him for a little while. She wouldn't be able to concentrate on any real riding anyway after that dreadful conversation she had had.

She wondered what Pester had said to Steve. Was she going to write about him as well? If Pester had reacted when she saw Steve lose his patience with his old horse it perhaps wasn't surprising. But what that had to do with her, Sara, she couldn't understand. She had herself talked to Steve once or twice about perhaps going a little easier on his horse, which was no longer so young. It was very well trained but didn't always share Steve's view on how things should be done. Steve really wasn't a bad chap, but sometimes he became impatient and irritated when the horse didn't do what he asked. Then he might use both his stick and his spurs in a rather unpleasant way. There were a lot of people who had seen him do that.

Sara had even on one occasion asked him if she could try and get his horse to do what it was refusing so obstinately to do when Steve rode it. Steve, who naturally wanted to learn, had thankfully accepted her help and acknowledged that it worked much better when you didn't use force. He was young and ambitious and sometimes a little too keen to make progress quickly, which was not always such a good idea when you were dealing with animals. But he was a good rider and Sara was convinced that in the future he would realize that if he could just master his temper, the progress would come.

But if Pester had reacted to Steve's way of riding and even had the temerity to suggest that Sara had done something inappropriate, Sara couldn't then understand why Pester hadn't reacted in the riding school to what was going on? Watching the unfortunate school horses trotting round for hours with people on their backs who were constantly off beat and who kicked the horses in the ribs at the same time as they pulled on the reins was not an edifying sight. The riding pupils were not unkind but they quite simply found it difficult to keep their balance. But the horses didn't know that and they looked more and more unhappy by the day as they were obliged to suffer these lessons. Not one hour a day, not even two or three, but four, five hours–every day! What's more their heads were pulled down with a fixed extra rein, just so that they wouldn't protest too strongly.

Why didn't Eve Pester react and write about that, wondered Sara. She could really have done something for those poor horses. Sara was convinced that there were school horses up and down the country who had an even worse life. The riding club where Sara rode was considered one of the best in Sweden and it was also one of the biggest. In general it was accepted that the horses had quite a good life there. Even if that evidently didn't mean a lot.

Sara took Mozart into the indoor school and mounted. There was another rider there already, Rita Johnson. Sara told her what had happened. They rode side by side and Sara repeated the conversation she had had with Pester. Rita tried to comfort her: 'But what can she write? You haven't done anything! She said so herself–she hadn't seen you hit any horse. She had only heard allegations from other people. Surely she can't write about that!' Rita continued until Sara felt a bit more cheerful. No, she hadn't done anything, so what could Pester actually write about?

But what had she meant by saying that there were 'brave' people who dared to stand up and tell what they had seen? In herself she knew that they couldn't have 'seen' anything at all, since she hadn't done anything. But on the other hand that meant that these 'brave' people could tell Pester exactly what they wanted, and that she believed them. Sara was convinced she knew who the 'brave' people were.

After a while Steve too came into the manege with his horse. When he had mounted he tried to make a bit of a joke of it: 'Soon we won't even dare to get on a horse without being accused of cruelty to animals.' He didn't look particularly happy about his conversation with Pester either. Sara couldn't bring herself to answer, she was still shocked about what Pester had said to her. And she couldn't for a moment imagine how anyone had got a journalist from one of the biggest papers in Sweden to listen to them at all, much less write something to suit their purpose.

Admittedly Pester had more than once grabbed the headlines to whip up a scandal. Sara remembered how some months earlier Pester had accused one of the national show-jumping riders of going around and competing on a lame horse. Naturally there wasn't a shred of truth in it but if Pester said it was so, it didn't help even if both the national team trainer and the vet said it wasn't. She had a habit of taking no notice of riders or vets, judges or trainers, riding managers or competition organizers. The whole thing had fizzled out but Pester had got her headlines.

What Sara couldn't understand was Pester's evident hatred of her. Sara had felt this before, when she had come across the journalist once or twice. It had always been just as uncomfortable, even when Pester had not spoken to her directly. Sara only had to see her in the distance to feel shivers down her spine. She could never understand why.

Sara finished her walking turn with Mozart. He hadn't had a lot of exercise but she couldn't bring herself to ride any longer. She felt she had to get home to her family. Her whole being was in tumult. She couldn't hold back her despair much longer. She patted her horse and put him in his box; he would be ridden by Lou at the weekend anyway.

When Sara got home and told Martin, Erwin and her mother about her conversation with Pester, they consoled her as well as they could. And they couldn't understand either how a journalist could express herself as she had. They were absolutely convinced that there wouldn't be any big headlines, because there was nothing to write about.

That night was the beginning of a new phase in Sara's life. Doors would open up to her which she had believed were closed for ever. Doors which had been open a chink when she was a child, but which had gradually closed completely as the years had passed. Now they were mercilessly thrown open again. And behind those doors there was a hell waiting for her which could not even be imagined. She would look into the abyss in a way which was absolutely incomprehensible, and her life would hang by a very fine thread.

15

Faces from the past

She is back in the house of fear. She is so frightened that she feels the fear in every fibre of her body. She hasn't done anything to deserve being hunted like this. It is a completely unjustified 'hunt' in which all her rights are taken from her.

She shrinks down on the floor and tries to make herself as small as possible. In her hands she is grasping her book with the red cover. Her heart is beating so loudly she can hear it and she is trying in vain to hold back her tears. She cries aloud when someone grabs her by the neck and pulls her out. The book slides across the floor as she is pulled up and held with an iron grip round her neck.

She is so terrified that her legs give way under her. As she is pushed down the stairs she falls on the bottom step and just lies there. In terror she looks up at her tormentor. His eyes glow with hatred and he drags her up by the hair. 'Get up you damned slut.' He goes on pulling her by the hair out on to the street and into a waiting black car. She screams as she sees his face and recognizes him.

Sara woke from her own screaming. She had been crying her eyes out and she still couldn't stop crying even though she was awake. She remembered everything from her dream down to the smallest detail. In shock, and on shaking legs, she got out of bed and went to the kitchen. She tried to drink a little milk but she couldn't stop shaking.

Sara sat down and hid her face in her hands, weeping. What was happening? How could she remember him from the past, even though he looked so different? How could she recognize him? Why were these memories coming back? After all these years? Why had that door been opened to her again? Why couldn't she be allowed to forget? All these questions, to which there were no answers, were driving her mad. Her head was splitting and she didn't dare go and lie down again for several hours. In the end she stumbled back to her bed and fell on it in an exhausted heap.

No matter how Sara tried to prepare herself for Pester's attack, she could never have imagined what happened next. Early in the morning she was up to get the paper when it arrived. On the front page she saw the headline 'RIDER ACCUSED OF CRUELTY TO ANIMALS.' With trembling hands Sara opened the paper. As she flicked through it she suddenly stopped. She was absolutely white in the face and she recoiled as the article met her eyes. A full page article trumpeted: 'HOW LONG MUST THESE HORSES SUFFER?'

Pester's article told of Steve whom she had seen kicking and hitting his horse, but also of Sara, the former mounted police officer. Pester described in detail how she had seen with her own eyes Sara ill-treating both her sponsored horse Mozart and a pupil's horse. Pester had visited the riding club herself a few days earlier and now she could reveal what went on when people rode so-called dressage. She described how Sara 'pulled, sawed at and kicked the poor horses until they were totally worn down, and how it was frightening that there were people who placed horses in the hands of a person like Sara. And as if that were not enough, this had been going on for many years. Among other things there was one poor stallion who on one occasion had had a taste of Sara's cruelty!

The fact that the Riding Federation had even agreed to sponsor her with a horse was horrifying. The 'brave' people had come forward, Veronica and two of the riding school instructors. They told how shocked they were that they had to watch Sara every day and see how she treated the poor horses. For a long time they had tried to get the board to exclude her from the Riding Club. What Pester had seen was by no means exceptional. Every day riding pupils were thrown off and injured because Sara was whipping the life out of her horse. Now they simply couldn't put up with it any longer.

Sara read while the tears ran. An abyss was opening up. It felt as if the earth was cracking beneath her feet. She could not believe that this was really happening. Was she still dreaming? Was this too a nightmare from which she would awake screaming?

No, reality was all too tangible, the article lay there in front of her. The words cut her like knives, but she was compelled to continue reading. The article concluded with a demand from Pester that the Riding Federation should immediately take Mozart away from Sara and place him with some other rider.

Sara collapsed on the floor. Martin, who was by now over twenty years old, sat down with her. He hugged her and tried to comfort her as best he could. Sara's mother and Erwin were also absolutely in despair. They did everything they could to infuse courage into Sara. 'Everybody knows that this is lies and malicious slander. Nobody can possibly believe it.'

Sara listened to them but their words couldn't reach her. She just sat there still on the floor and the tears ran. The despair she felt now knew no bounds. She didn't believe that she had the strength to live another minute. But Martin would not give up, he talked and talked. He did not leave her for a second. In the end his words began to penetrate her consciousness. Hours later the tears had dried and her brain could begin to function again.

She knew now that Pester would do everything in her power to fulfil her promise: to put an end to her and her riding. What she could not get her head around was what it was that could drive Pester to do this?

Later in the afternoon, when Sara came to the Horse Show with Mozart, she was met with looks which terrified her. People she met looked at her with hatred or turned their faces away. There was no doubt that people had read Pester's article and what was more believed it. Sara sought out Lou as quickly as she could to tell her that Mozart was there ready. Lou looked almost embarrassed: 'Good Lord Sara, what have you done to upset Pester? It's the most terrible thing I've ever read!' Lou held up the newspaper. Sara didn't know how she should reply. It seemed absolutely pointless to say, 'I've done nothing.' You couldn't be written about like that without having done anything—under normal circumstances. Once or twice previously Sara had told Lou about how she had been treated in the Mounted Police and later at the Riding Club. But to try and explain everything that had happened now was just impossible. Sara contented herself with saying that perhaps they could talk about it quietly somewhere later.

People who passed by as they were standing there talking looked at Lou with looks which said, 'How can you stand and talk to that horse abuser?' Lou looked noticeably uncomfortable. Even though she undoubtedly felt sorry for Sara, she didn't like people giving her looks like that either. She broke off the conversation and said that it would be better for them to talk about it later. Sara understood Lou completely. But at that moment she felt like the loneliest person on earth. People were swarming around her. She knew a lot of them but they looked away when they saw her. Some of them looked at her with obvious disgust. They pointed and whispered around her, but not one of them came up to her where she stood alone.

Sara realized that she now had to decide for herself whether Pester, Veronica, Ulrich and the others who were persecuting her should be allowed to succeed in their attempts to crush her. The alternative was to fight to clear her name. In fact the choice was not difficult. She knew in her heart that she only had one option and that was not to give in and give up. She didn't have a clue how she would manage it. But she was absolutely determined to fight her persecutors as long as she possibly could and had the strength to do it.

She pulled herself together and went back to Mozart where he was stabled. On the way she greeted people she knew as if nothing had happened. Some looked extremely embarrassed, but she pretended she hadn't noticed. She put on a cheerful face, but she was weeping inwardly.

'Hi, haven't seen you for ages!' It was a woman police officer from another town who was cheerfully saying hello.

'She can't have read the article,' that was Sara's first thought when she returned her greeting.

'How are you? It's terrible, this attack on you in the newspaper.' Her colleague looked really sorry and continued: 'Don't you think there is something you can do about that Pester woman? She really must have gone well beyond the bounds of what's acceptable this time surely?'

Sara, who had managed to hold her head high and keep back the tears when everybody had looked despisingly and angrily at her, burst into tears. She had seen people who had been her friends for many years, people who had looked away and turned their backs on her when she had greeted them. Now there was a person in front of her whom she had met fleetingly at a few police competitions and who hugged her as she sobbed out all her despair. She was ashamed that she couldn't control herself and tried to apologize between the tears.

'You really don't have to say sorry.' The woman police officer gave her a handkerchief and hugged her. 'It's quite natural you should cry. I would probably have broken down completely if I had been attacked like you. The fact that you can walk here with your head high shows incredible strength, and you should carry on like that. Don't let them grind you down. You have a lot of friends, even though it maybe doesn't feel like it just now.'

Sara, who had cried her eyes out, dried her face frantically and tried to pull herself together. It was so unexpected to meet someone offering her kindness and compassion. She was absolutely overwhelmed. She had steeled herself to meet nasty looks and frosty comments. As she felt the warmth now emanating to her from her colleague, she just couldn't handle it. They went their separate ways after Sara had promised to continue to stand up for herself and not give up. 'You have a lot of friends who are thinking of you, don't you forget it!' were the last words Sara heard before she disappeared into the sea of people. When she got back to Mozart in the temporary stable, she met Lou again. She had obviously been waiting for Sara to come. 'Sara I'm afraid I can't ride Mozart in the display. The Federation has told me it wouldn't be appropriate.' Sara was completely dumbstruck. She looked uncomprehendingly at Lou. 'I'm sorry but there's nothing I can do about it. But I'll be happy to ride him in the early mornings these next few days anyway, so let him stay here.' Lou looked sympathetically at Sara and tipped her head to one side: 'Look, keep your chin up, this isn't the end of the world. It'll soon blow over, you'll see. I'll ride Mozart in the training periods in the morning, so everyone can see that I haven't given up on you or him.'

Sara felt somewhat relieved. Driving Mozart back to the Riding Club and being forced to ride him there herself the whole weekend wasn't something she could cope with, she could feel that. She thanked Lou and left Mozart behind.

On her way out she met the Riding Federation Secretary, Bud Mudie. He pretended he didn't see her, even though she was standing a couple of feet from him.

'Hello, sorry to bother you but I would like to talk to you, if you have the time?' She was surprised that he hadn't taken the initiative. He looked at his watch and seemed stressed. 'I'm in a bit of a hurry just now. But you'll be getting a letter from me after the weekend. You'll get your chance to put your point of view.'

They went their separate ways. Although Sara was disappointed at Mudie's distant attitude, she still felt a bit more hopeful. She was going to get a chance to tell them how things really were.

That evening the telephone rang continuously. Her colleague had been right, Sara had a lot of friends. Real friends who were shocked by Pester's hateful attack. They tried to cheer her up and support her and Sara felt their warmth flowing towards her. It was like balm to her aching soul. She treasured every encouraging word her friends gave her.

Her pupil, Joo Bergman, who owned the horse which Pester claimed she had seen ill-treated, rang up. 'Surely it can't be my horse that Pester's written about, can it?' When Sara assured her that it really was, she thought Joo would explode! 'Pester must be out of her mind! Tomorrow morning I'm going to ring her myself first thing, that's for sure. She lies as easily as a horse trots. I was there every second you were riding. My horse went better than ever before.' Sara listened to her and tried to get a word in edgeways: 'Joo, I tried to talk to Pester before she published the article. It didn't make any difference what I said. She even acknowledged that it was one of my better days, but that she knew what happened when no one was watching me.' Sara was resigned, although naturally she appreciated Joo's involvement. Joo was decided, of course it must be possible to talk to Pester? She, Joo, was after all the owner of the horse in question! Sara wished her luck.

Bob Nelson, another friend of Sara's, rang too and was extremely upset. He told her that he had actually been at the riding club at the same time as Pester. He had stood by a window looking out over the indoor school where Sara was riding. He had also noticed Pester there. Now he was wondering what on earth she thought she was doing? He couldn't understand how Pester, who was a well-known journalist, dared to lie and publish such obviously false allegations. Especially when they were of such a serious nature. Bob had followed the whole of Sara's turn and he knew that there had not even been one hard jerk on the reins.

Naturally Sara felt extremely relieved that there were two completely independent people who had seen her riding. But she had an uncomfortable feeling that it might not help. Pester had incredible power. She was obviously in a position to write what she felt like.

That evening, after so many phone calls and a lot of tears, Sara was absolutely exhausted. She dropped into bed and fell asleep immediately. But she was not going to get any rest. The other hell broke over her again.

Once again she looks into his eyes. Time seems to stand still as

their eyes meet. Her eyes, big, brown, filled with fear and confu-
sion. His, ice-cold, steel grey and triumphant. She screams out...

Her own scream of fear woke her and she flew up out of the
bed. She was on the verge of hysteria. It felt as if the whole of
her inner being would explode.

One hell by day and another by night. And yet in some way
they belonged together. Sara didn't know what to do with
herself. She was beginning to lose her grip completely. Earlier
in her life, when she had had her memories, she had always
been able to turn back to her safe and real world again. But
now it felt as if it was collapsing around her. And the dreams
were just getting more intense and more real...

There was no more sleep for Sara that night.

In the morning she heard the newspaper fall through the
letterbox. When she bent down to pick it up, it was with a faint
hope that there would at least be a retraction, an admission
that Pester had not herself seen Sara ill-treat any horse, that it
was only hearsay and that the people who had made the
allegations had to defend them. For surely a paper couldn't let
one of its journalists take a completely one-sided view and
what's more even do other people's dirty work for them?

When she reached the sports pages, she realized that she
had been mistaken. Another full page article met her eyes:
'RIDING FEDERATION MUST DO SOMETHING!' The article under this
headline was just as thoroughly hateful as that of the previous
day. Pester also reported how many people had rung her up
and thanked her for getting something done at last.

Only one person, Bob Nelson, had rung and put a different
viewpoint. He was quoted: 'I think Sara's riding is OK.' The
text which followed gave the impression that Bob Nelson
thought it was perfectly all right to ill-treat horses when you
rode them.

Sara read and wept in turn. She knew she shouldn't read any more but she still couldn't bring herself to push this evil thing away from her. It overwhelmed her like a big roaring monster. She felt the fear creeping through her body. The evil was so tangible that she could almost touch it. How could she possibly defend herself against it?

Later in the day Joo rang. Sara could hardly understand what she was saying, she was talking so fast. 'She's completely out of her mind, that Pester woman. She threatened me, she really did.' Joo stumbled over her words. Sara tried to get her to calm down so that she could hear what she was saying. Joo took a deep breath and began to tell her: 'First of all she told me that I should be ashamed of letting you ride my horse. I should have realized for myself that this would happen when I asked you for help. She immediately ordered me to change trainers and use one of the riding instructors at the Club. On top of that she warned me that something might happen to me if I took your side. I was really frightened, I can tell you.' Sara realized that Pester had really given Joo a hard time.

'But I know what I know. I'll take the consequences, whatever Pester threatens me with.' Joo sounded determined and Sara understood that she wouldn't allow herself to be frightened into saying something that was not true.

Bob also contacted Sara. He was completely overcome. He repeated the conversation he had had with Pester and naturally he had said what she quoted in a completely different context. He realized that it was absolutely pointless to try and talk to her. She was not interested for a moment in hearing anything good about Sara. 'If you decide to take legal action against Pester and her paper, you know I want to testify and tell them the truth.'

They talked for a while about how incomprehensible

Pester's behaviour was before they ended their conversation. Admittedly all the support she was getting comforted Sara greatly but she was so devastated by what was happening that she didn't know how she was going to survive to the next day. And the next...

It was not just the daily hell she had to fight. She was terrified of going to bed when night came. Just imagine if the door to that other abyss were to open up again? She wouldn't be able to meet his eyes, and feel his hands on her neck once again, that she was absolutely sure of.

16

The hunt continues

But the night came and the dream with it.

The iron grip around her neck is merciless. She is dragged into a black car and he sits beside her. She can feel how his hands are groping under her jumper. He gets hold of one of her breasts, at the same time pushing her face down on to his knee.

Wild with rage and fear she swings round. She is fighting for her life, it feels as if she will die any second. Suddenly he lifts her by the hair and hits her full in the face. She feels it burning and blood pours from her nose. He pushes her down on to the floor.

Sara woke up. For a moment she didn't know whether she was in the present or the past. She could still feel the blow and how her face was burning. Her whole body felt shattered. Blood was dripping from her nose and she went out to the bathroom and looked at herself in the mirror. She recoiled in fear as she saw the blood running and what her face looked like. The nightmare was just as real as the one in the daytime. Sara collapsed on the bathroom floor and cried and cried.

Morning came. Sara woke up on the floor where she had fallen asleep out of pure exhaustion. Her nose had stopped bleeding, but she felt bruised all over from the struggles of the night. She didn't know what to do with herself. What was happening? Why were these memories flooding over her again? And why were they so mercilessly real? She tried to find answers. Could it be that she was now about to settle her account with that terrifying past time once and for all? Had the people who were involved in the persecution then not fulfilled their evil intent? Was there a direct connection to her previous life? Was it the same souls which were pursuing her, then and now? The same souls in different bodies, unrecognizable to her? Until now?

If it was so, Sara realized, she would have to dare to confront these people and try to vanquish their hatred. Otherwise they would continue their hunt until they had managed to destroy her, just as they had decided in their souls to do. But she still couldn't understand what it was that was driving them to attack her so determinedly and ruthlessly. Why were they so blind in their hatred? And what could she do to be free of them? So many questions and not a single answer.

Sara avoided reading the paper that morning. The Easter weekend and the Horse Show were in full swing. She pulled herself together and drove there to see Mozart and spend a little time with him.

She was scarcely inside the door when she met someone she only knew fleetingly. 'Isn't it awful, that article Pester's written about you in today's paper! It'll take a lot for you to get out of this unscathed.' He didn't look particularly sorry. Sara's stomach turned over, but she replied as indifferently as she could that she hadn't read the paper yet.

She rushed down to Mozart in the stable. She couldn't hold back the tears. 'Amadeus', she called to him when she was still just too far away for him to see her. He answered her immediately with a loud neigh. She rushed in to him and shut the box door so that nobody could see her tear-stained face. She sat down in the corner and Amadeus nuzzled her hair and face. He could feel how sad she was and that things were not right.

He nudged her gently to try and get her back to normal again but she just went on weeping. He became really worried. He stood with his nose pressed close against her and waited for her to become herself again.

Sara didn't know how long she had sat there when she heard her friends, Lou and the other dressage riders, walk into the stable. She got up and turned her face towards Amadeus when they came up to the box. She was ashamed to let them see how sad she was. They all thought she was strong, that she wasn't one to give up and cry uncontrollably. They exchanged a few words, but sensitive as they were, they understood that she wanted to be alone with her horse.

When Sara got home Bob rang. He thought, after reading Pester's third article, that she should contact a lawyer who could help her to put a stop to the paper's lies. She agreed with him that she needed help. But was there really anyone who didn't know her but who would nonetheless believe in her? And could she afford to hire a lawyer? It didn't seem likely. But Bob insisted and gave her the telephone number of a lawyer he had heard of. He was said to specialize precisely in cases involving the freedom of the press.

Sara looked at the piece of paper with the telephone number several times that day and in the end she dialled the number. 'Alec Peterson.' His voice sounded kind and Sara introduced herself. She explained why she had rung and what Pester had written. When she had finished there was no sound from the other end of the line.

Sara wondered if he was still there? 'Yes, I'm here.' She could hear that his tone had changed now. Somewhat guarded and curt. She still continued her story unhesitatingly and didn't stop until she had told him everything. The seconds before she received any reply seemed long, but finally he

answered a little guardedly that she could send him the arti
cles and a summary of what had happened.

'I can't promise you that I can do anything but I will get in
touch when I have gone through your papers.' Before they
hung up he recommended Sara to ask a vet to look at Mozart
and give an opinion as to whether the horse had been ill-
treated or not. Sara promised to do exactly what he said. As
soon as she had put down the receiver she rang the vet. He
promised to come out straight after Easter and inspect Mozart.
Sara picked up that day's newspaper with the blaring headline
'ACCUSED TRAINERS EXPELLED'. The text said that she and Steve
had been expelled and banned by the Club directors from
training pupils on their premises. 'Both the Riding Federation
and the Club directors have taken firm action since our
revelations about the ill-treated horses.'

She couldn't bear to read any more. But she cut out the
article and put it with the other three in an envelope, which
she was going to send to Alec Peterson. She laid the paper
aside and tried to put what she had read out of her mind. She
wasn't very successful and once again the tears began to flow
without her being able to stop them.

The Easter weekend was over and a letter came from the
Riding Federation addressed to Sara. She ripped it open. 'I
would appreciate your view of the articles which have been
published in the newspaper over the Easter weekend. I look
forward to receiving your written reply within a week. Yours
sincerely, Bud Mudie.'

Sara sat down at the typewriter immediately. Now at last she
would be able to tell the Federation what was behind all this. It
was a long letter but it was necessary to get everything in. She
wrote about her time in the Mounted Police and about the post

she had applied for. She also felt compelled to tell them about the Riding Club, how the financial side of the business had been operating and how in the end her perseverance had resulted in an audit which had revealed that thousands of crowns had gone missing. But the most important of all was that she was able to write about how crazy the allegations against her were. She explained where they came from and how they had begun several years earlier.

When she had finished there were eleven pages, but there was nothing she could leave out. It was vital to her that the Riding Federation should understand the connection and realize that she really was innocent of all these terrible charges. As she stuck down the envelope she felt a little hopeful, for the first time since the nightmare had begun. It had been good to write and tell all. Now they must understand how things really were. Perhaps the Riding Federation would help her to get all this dreadful business put right?

Later the same day Sara had a conversation with the vet. She met him in the stable yard. 'I can understand why you want an inspection; these things you're accused of are no joke.' He looked sympathetically at her as she went to fetch Mozart. The vet examined him thoroughly. Sara wanted the certificate to be as detailed as possible anyway. There must be no doubt that her beloved horse was in perfect condition. 'Please check his sides and mouth extra carefully, since they are claiming that I have kicked his sides with my spurs and pulled at his mouth.'

When the examination was completed, the vet looked kindly at Sara: 'Well now, just imagine if all the horses looked like this—I would be out of a job. Your horse is in perfect condition, both physically and mentally.' Sara received the certificate from him and for a brief moment felt cheered by these heartening words.

17

Dark times

The days passed and Sara waited to hear from Bud Mudie, in response to her letter. Finally she couldn't wait any longer and she rang him up.

'You mean that long letter?' he wondered. Sara agreed that it was long and asked if he had read it.

'No, I couldn't manage to read it, it was much too long.' He didn't sound particularly friendly and he continued: 'I have passed it on to the Disciplinary Board instead. They'll have to decide what to do.'

Sara was completely at a loss. She wondered what he was talking about? How could he do that without even reading what she had written to him? With horror she realized what an enormous impact Pester had had.

'Admittedly you haven't been reported for any offence. But if nobody else is going to do anything, I'll report you myself on the basis of the articles.' His voice was cold and impersonal.

Sara didn't know whether she was awake or in the grip of a nightmare. Could this be real? The conversation was ended and Sara put down the receiver with a shaking hand. 'Disciplinary Board?' 'Report me?' 'Couldn't manage to read it.' Her head was spinning. She thought she would go mad. She took a copy of her letter to Mudie and put it in an envelope for Alec Peterson. She had already sent him the articles and the vet's certificate.

Pester didn't let up. With only a few days interval between, she published one article after another. She wasn't writing so much about Steve now, she was concentrating entirely on Sara.

Sara dragged herself about more or less in shock. She cried more during those days than she had cried in the whole of her life. It felt as if evil was consuming her from within. She tried to keep up appearances as best she could and live normally as far as possible.

Almost all her pupils left her, with the explanation that it was hard to have to account for themselves if they carried on training with her. None of them had ever seen Sara do anything which was even remotely like what she was accused of, but there was so much stuff in the newspaper that there must surely be something in it?

Even though it was a financial disaster for her, she didn't for one moment try to persuade anyone to continue to rely on her. If they couldn't cope with the stress involved in taking her side, and chose instead to howl with the wolves, it wasn't something she could do anything about. She was very much saddened by it, not so much for the money but because she had really believed that they would stick up for her. She remembered how several of them had expressed their gratitude only a few weeks previously for the way she had solved their problems. How they had said it was so nice to have finally found a trainer who didn't reach for the stick and harsh words when things didn't go right. But now all that was forgotten.

Sara was in her car on her way home from the stables. She stopped at a red light and in passing glanced at the bill boards by the news stand. One of them shone out like a beacon, and she was rooted to the spot in the car long after the lights had turned green. 'ANIMAL ABUSER CONFESSES.'

From a long way away she heard cars hooting. Finally she pulled herself together and pulled in to the kerb. On shaking legs she crossed the street, went up to the stand and bought the paper. When she came back to the car she sat down and read.

Both the front page and half a page inside the paper claimed to be able to report to their readers that one of the animal abusers had confessed. Steve had written to the Riding Federation and begged pardon for his behaviour. He had acknowledged that he had been too hard on his horse. Pester noted this and was pleased that Steve had apologized. The remainder of the article was devoted to Sara and what a shame it was that she couldn't display the same courage and stand up and admit what she had done.

When Sara had finished reading she was not capable of driving another yard. She sat there for hours, totally annihilated. Finally she started the car and drove slowly home.

That was still not the end of it: in all the evening papers people could read about the mounted police officer and woman dressage rider who abused her horses and refused to admit it. At least the other rider had been strong and acknowledged what he had done. It was included in the news on the radio and there was even an item on TV in the late programme.

Sara fell into a deep black hole. It felt as if she would never get out of it again. Everything was spinning around her. Lightning images whirled past on her way down into the abyss. Images from a forgotten time. She screamed out. Her lungs had to provide an escape for all her pain. The pain which she had borne within her since the previous time she had visited the earth also overwhelmed her at that moment. Now all the terror and the helplessness came to the surface. Her heart beat faster and faster and within her everything was total chaos.

She didn't know how long she had been in that state when she came to herself again. Martin was sitting there holding her in his arms. He was rocking her like a little child and she felt his indescribable love and his despair. He wouldn't let her go until she was completely calm. He helped her to lie down on the sofa and spread a blanket over her. Then he sat down and played the piano. He played a wonderful classical piece which soothed her wounded soul.

In despair Sara put her hands together and begged for help to get through this hell and be freed from her persecutors. She thanked the Supreme Force for the greatest gift which life had given her, her son. Finally she fell asleep and was able to sleep without any nocturnal shadows chasing her.

The following morning Alec Peterson rang. He thanked her for her letter with the articles and the vet's certificate. The copy of her letter to Bud Mudie had also reached him. 'This is a terrible mess you've landed in.' He sounded kind. Sara held her breath. Could he help her? Or rather, would he want to help her?

'I've decided that I believe in you, and I'm going to see what I can do to help you.'

Sara felt like a drowning man who has been thrown a life-belt. They talked for a while and agreed that Sara would keep him informed about Pester's writings. Alec thought it might be possible to take some action against the newspaper for what Pester had already written but he didn't want to do anything too hastily. He wanted to see how things developed first.

Sara felt complete faith in the voice at the other end of the line. Alec Peterson sounded like an 'old soul'. By that Sara meant a person who cared about right and wrong, who believed in justice, and who wanted to help a fellow human being. Naturally he had to be paid for his work; after all it was his bread and butter. After their conversation Sara was glad she had taken Bob's advice to ring Alec.

The days passed. Sometimes there was a fresh article in the paper about her, signed Eve Pester. Sara tried to keep her distance from what she read, and instead pass everything on to Alec.

But her mother read everything. In the end *she* couldn't take any more. Her mother's heart just couldn't stand any more grief. In the nick of time the ambulance came and her life was saved by a hair's breadth. Sara's despair and fear of losing her mother, who meant everything to her, awoke a hatred in her which she had never thought herself capable of feeling.

She knew that she would be forced to stand up to her persecutors and rid herself of them. How that would be possible she had no idea. Her prayers had never been as intense as now, when she sat beside that sick-bed and saw her mother fighting for her life.

18

Frightened—and alone

Sara's mother had to stay in hospital, but after a few weeks she was out of danger. The relief Sara felt when the doctor gave her the good news was enormous. If her mother had left her she would not have had the strength to go on living, that she knew. Her mother was and always had been her greatest security. They had a very special relationship. Mother and child are always close of course but Sara and her mother had a spiritual bond between them.

Always, in all the phases of their life, they had been very close to one another. Sara really couldn't conceive of life without her mother. And that was not just because her mother had bound her to her. No, she had never ever demanded anything of Sara. Sara had never heard her mother say 'But what about me, can't I have...'

Everything her mother did in this life was unselfish and loving. That was undoubtedly what had led to her heart not being able to cope any longer in the end, thought Sara. Her mother had not been able to feel any wrath about the misfortunes Sara had had to face—only grief. Intense and overwhelming grief. Wrath to her was an alien, unknown concept. Sara thanked the Supreme Force that her prayers had not remained unanswered.

Time passed. Sara heard nothing from the Riding Federation. The last sign of life from them had been the telephone conversation she had had with Bud Mudie. Whatever else she knew she had read in the paper. Finally she wrote a letter to the Disciplinary Board, which Mudie said had received her letter. She asked whether she had been reported for anything? And if so what?

Once again she waited in vain for a reply. In the end she rang the Riding Federation. The Disciplinary Board seemed so complex to her that she didn't know which person she should contact there. She got hold of the Chief Officer for Sports, Ian Borg. He told her that the Disciplinary Board was to process 'the case', as he called it, within the next few days. She could ring one of the members of the Board, John Meadow, when they had reached a decision, so that she could find out their ruling.

Sara couldn't understand what the Chief Officer was talking about at all. What 'case'? Sara asked what he meant. How could a Disciplinary Board have a meeting when they had not even investigated what it was all about? Nobody had talked to her. Sara's questions remained unanswered. Borg repeated that she would have to wait until she could talk to one of the members of the Board. She waited a few days and then rang the number she had been given for John Meadow. He took the call himself. Sara introduced herself and told him why she was ringing. She wondered whether they had had any meeting about her? They had but she couldn't be told what they had decided since it was not official yet. It was still confidential. In five days' time a press release would be issued. She could ring him in the morning of the same day.

Sara thought she was dreaming. If they really had made a decision now, without even talking to her first, was she really expected to wait five days before being told anything? Couldn't he even tell her what she was accused of, more specifically than what was apparent from Pester's rambling articles? No! John Meadow refused to give her any information whatsoever. She would have to wait 'like everybody else' as he expressed it.

Late that evening the telephone rang at Sara's home. It was Bud Mudie. He now told her everything which John Meadow had claimed was confidential just a few hours earlier. The Board had acquitted Steve, since he had confessed. But as regards Sara things were not so good. She had not confessed. They were now going to collect witness statements so that they could judge her. His actual purpose in ringing was not that at all. He just wanted to tell her that she had to refrain from taking part in competitions with Mozart until 'everything was settled'.

When Sara tried in vain to get him to explain what the Board meant by saying that Steve was acquitted but not her, he dismissed her question. She wondered whether she was barred from competitions? No, not officially. But Mudie wanted to make her aware that it was not appropriate ... Sara realized that she would do best not to protest but to accept his 'plea'. After all she only owned one third of the horse herself. There was a certain risk that that could change.

The next morning Sara read yet another article by Pester. Parts of it were a summary of the conversation she had had with Bud Mudie the evening before. He was cited: 'Sara herself agreed with me that it would be inappropriate for her to compete with the horse in the present circumstances.' After the quotation Pester had made it seem as though Sara herself had realized that she couldn't compete with a horse which was so run down.

As arranged, five days later Sara rang John Meadow. She pretended not to know anything. Evidently he had no knowledge at all of the well-informed sources of the press. He told her everything that Sara had already read in the press a few days earlier. When he had finished, Sara asked if there was nothing he could tell her which she hadn't already read in Pester's latest article?

There was an awkward silence for a long moment until, in a strained voice, he asked her what she meant?

'Precisely what I said' replied Sara, 'everything you have just told me I was told by Bud Mudie the same evening that I had talked to you. The next day it was all there in Pester's article for everyone to read.' She heard him draw in his breath. 'This is not good,' he muttered and Sara understood that he was anxious to conclude their conversation.

The decision which the Board had reached really beggared belief. Sara realized that as she read the press release. Since Steve had admitted that he had hit his horse, they could acquit him. They had ruled that the reputation of the sport had not suffered and therefore Steve could not be punished.

Sara was naturally pleased for Steve but she couldn't help wondering what joy his horse might have from knowing that the reputation of the sport had not been damaged? They had not been able to deal with Sara's 'case' since she insisted on denying her ill deeds. Her problem had suddenly become that she had not hit her horse! If she had done, she could have confessed and thus been acquitted.

The Disciplinary Board wrote a letter to Veronica and the riding instructors at the Club and asked them to submit specific accusations so that Sara could be disciplined. Pester could now at last concentrate on what she had intended from the start: putting an end to Sara and her riding. Now the witch hunt began in earnest. In the next article Pester and Mudie spoke out together and challenged people to show their courage and report Sara, so that she could receive her just punishment.

Sara's life was beginning to seem more and more like a real nightmare. When she read their challenge and saw how Veronica was given space in the article to tell how desperate she was when nothing was done about Sara's cruelty to animals, then her darkest nightmares became a reality.

That night was to be the worst of all her nightmare nights so far. Now the whole situation would be laid bare. She would receive full insight into the underlying causes which hitherto had been so well concealed. The witch hunt was not a coincidence.

There is silence in the big room, apart from the breathing of the sleeping people lying around her. She can't sleep. Hunger gnaws at her stomach and she is constantly cold. And she is afraid. So unbearably afraid and alone. She weeps silently.

Now she can hear the footsteps again. They are coming closer and closer to her bunk. She makes herself as small as possible and crouches down. But it doesn't help now he has reached her. He pulls off the blanket covering her. His hands are all over her body and she feels that she is going to be sick. Although she knows he will hit her, she defends herself against his hands as if her life depended on it.

It is the same man who dragged her into the black car a few months before. She had been absolutely terrified when she saw him in the camp and learned that he had got a transfer there. Now he was one of the people who gave the orders.

'You damned Jewish slut, I'll make you stop this fighting for sure.' He hits her hard in the face and pushes her down under him.

She tries to scream but he has his hand tight over her mouth. 'Now we're going to carry on where we left off last time. You were so damned tough then but now perhaps you've calmed down a bit, hm?' His voice cuts her like a knife; she is fighting for her life.

Suddenly he drops her and stands up. Voices can be heard a little way away in the hut. There are two guards who've come round to check that everything is quiet. He leaves her with the words 'Don't worry, I'll be back. I always finish what I've started.'

The dream continues.

It's daytime and she is walking across a muddy yard when she is stopped by a woman's voice. 'Halt.' She stops but doesn't turn round. The woman guard comes up behind her. 'Just you wait. I know how you're baiting your trap to catch a man. One day I'll put an end to you once and for all.'

Sara recognizes the words and the voice. The woman is crazy because her male bedmate disappears night after night and doesn't come back for several hours. She has followed him and seen how he creeps away to the hut where that little Jewish cat is. What she hasn't seen is how violently the girl has defended herself and how he has had to give up so far. The reason he is sometimes away for several hours is that he goes on and creeps in to some other welcoming bosom in some other hut.

But the woman guard is convinced that it's that Jewish piece who has turned her man's head. More than once she has tried to get rid of her. So far she hasn't managed it but if she only gets the chance the girl is going to be eliminated. She just can't stand the sight of her.

No matter how she is oppressed, there is something inside her which no one can reach. A natural inner peace, which no one can shake. It makes the woman guard wild with fury, the fact that she can't extinguish the hope which burns in the girl's eyes. She raises her hand to strike...

'Mum, wake up! You're having a terrible dream.'

She is woken by Martin who is shaking her. He had heard from his room how she was calling out. It sounded as though she was terrified so he rushed in to her. When he saw her tossing back and forth in her bed, he knew he had to wake her up.

Sara was totally drained. Her bedclothes lay in a heap on the floor and she was bathed in sweat. When Martin hugged her and stroked her hair the tears came. She couldn't hold them back however hard she tried. The last thing she wanted was for him to see how despairing she was. But the experiences of that night had torn open a great wound inside her. She was so close to that time and that existence that she thought she couldn't keep that time and the present apart any longer.

'Thank you sweetheart, it's a good thing you woke me.' Sara tried to pull herself together and dried her tears. After a while she was able to pretend that she felt better. When Martin was sure that she was no longer upset he went back to his room. Then came the real shock of what she had experienced. Her whole body began to shake uncontrollably. How could she be rid of these creatures? Would she ever have an answer? Everything was spinning round. Finally she fell exhausted on her bed and slept until the morning.

The day passed. Sara was not in a fit state to do anything. She was panicking about the night to come and having to lie down and sleep again. She lay and read as long as she could but at last her eyes fell shut.

19

Back in hell

She is back in the yard. She is standing there alone in the dark. It is raining and she is soaked. Behind her is the same woman guard. Suddenly she is knocked to the ground. She lies there in the mud. When she tries to lift her face she can feel a shoe on her head, pressing her down. 'I'm going to see to it that those damned brown eyes are extinguished.' The words are hissed out, but Sara can hear them clearly. She doesn't dare to try and get up but lies quite still. Finally the foot pushing her down into the mud is lifted. She is yanked to her feet again.

Terrified, soaked to the skin and ice cold she looks at her oppressor. The features of the face and the look in the eyes are the same. And the voice. The seconds stand still.

'Stop looking at me I said.' The woman guard becomes totally hysterical as she sees the brown eyes looking at her. For one moment she seems to be considering what she's going to do, but then she turns and walks away.

The girl stands alone in the rain. She is crying and so cold that her whole emaciated body is shivering. But she doesn't intend to give up—ever. She is absolutely convinced that one day she will come home again. Home to her father's safe, warm embrace. Then everything will be like it was before again. Like it was before they had to hide in that terrible annexe and before they were carried off and separated. That hope and that faith help her to survive every day which comes.

She will never give up. All the evil which she has encountered and encounters daily must come to an end. It is Good which in the end must conquer. This is a conviction which she has always carried in her heart, ever since she was little. Nobody can make her give up that hope.

She goes back to the hut and her bunk. She takes her wet rags off. When she is completely naked she hears someone coming. She panics, but has no time to do anything before he is there in front of her.

'At last. Now you're not going to get away, I've been waiting for this.' He wrestles her down on to the bunk. The others, who have been woken by her cry, daren't say a word. All of them cower wordlessly; one sound and you're dead.

But suddenly that scene of terror changes. 'You damned Jewish whore. Now there'll be an end to you once and for all.' She is standing in the middle of the floor with her pistol aimed at them. Blind with rage and firmly convinced that the girl has turned her lover's head, she is at last going to put an end to the despicable whore. She raises the pistol, a shot is fired.

At the same moment he stands up. The bullet doesn't hit its target, it is stopped en route. He falls on top of the terrified girl. For one moment time stands still. There is a deathly silence after the pistol shot. The woman guard lowers her weapon when she realizes what she has done.

Now voices can be heard. Men yelling, feet running, dogs barking. Lamps are lit. Soon the whole hut is bathed in the light of searchlights and in a few seconds it is filled with men in uniform. She is still standing there in shock with the pistol in her hand when one of the men takes it away from her. He gives the order to arrest her. Now she gets her voice back. She hadn't intended him, her beloved, to die. It wasn't him she wanted to put an end to. It was a pure accident. She rambles incoherently.

But it doesn't matter what she says. The men in uniform are

filled with rage. She has killed one of them—and just because he wanted a bit of fun with one of his chattels. Naturally someone in his position had the right to take his pleasure where he liked. And this ugly woman guard hadn't been able to accept that.

They drag her out to the yard and throw her into the mud. She screams 'You can't do this to me, it's all that bloody Jewish whore's fault.' But nobody is listening to her. One of the men takes out his gun and aims it at the woman's head.

Just before the shot rings out, the woman swears a solemn oath. She will not rest until she has put out the light in that Jewish whore's ardent eyes. Before she is silenced by the death-bringing bullet, she shrieks out her curse.

The words are echoing in Sara's head when she wakes. It is early in the morning and the only sound is the cat purring next to her. She is shocked at what she has just experienced but she understands that it was necessary for her to know it. Finally she can see the connection and what lies behind the ruthless witch hunt of the present. Would she now be rid of these memories? Would she, through the knowledge she has now obtained, be able to put that time and that life behind her? Or were there more unexplained things she had to re-live? How far were these people prepared in their souls to go to carry out what they had made up their minds to do?

The questions crowded in upon her consciousness but she had no answers. Now she knew that what had happened and what was still happening were no coincidence. There was so much more behind it than anyone could have imagined in their wildest fantasy. Nor could she talk to anyone about it. Nobody would believe her if she tried to tell them. They would probably think that she had gone mad. She knew she would have to bear her knowledge within herself. The only one who might have been able to understand, and who she could have talked to, was her mother. But even though she was much better now, she was still in hospital, weak and vulnerable.

Although Sara visited her mother every day, she told her nothing of the terrors she experienced at night. The last thing she wanted was to upset her mother, who was fighting so bravely to get well again.

20

Accusations

Even though Sara couldn't tell her friends about these experiences, she couldn't ever have coped without them. Her true friends did everything they could to support her and help her as much as possible.

Jenny Best was such a friend. She was one of the most prestigious dressage riders in Sweden. For more than thirty years she had been the 'undisputed queen' of the dressage throne, with innumerable medals from various championships. Jenny was not afraid to show that she supported Sara, even though that meant that she got a 'going over' from Pester in the paper. Jenny had also boldly stated her views when Pester had rung her and tried to get her to see that she couldn't possibly support Sara. Jenny had asked Pester whether she had ever seen Sara hit a horse with a stick? Pester had admittedly not seen that, she acknowledged, but she wanted to warn Jenny and told her in confidence that Sara was a 'Dr. Jekyll and Mr. Hyde'.

After that conversation Jenny decided that something had to be done to draw the attention of the Riding Federation to the fact that it was unacceptable for a journalist to persecute an individual person in this way. She drafted a letter which the whole national dressage team signed. But it was too late; now things had gone so far that the Riding Federation had completely cracked up over Pester's repeated attacks in the newspaper.

Nobody gave a thought to Sara. They just wanted to make sure Pester got what she wanted so that she wouldn't attack the Riding Federation. Their strategy was that the best thing would be to throw the quarry to the wolves, so that perhaps they would stop howling. Nobody on the Riding Federation was bothered about the fact that it would mean the end for Sara. They didn't answer the letter from the national dressage team.

The next article was Pester's tenth about Sara. It repeated the same message as the earlier ones: Sara was cruel to animals. She had to be stopped from all riding, both training and competition. Her sponsored horse, Mozart, must be taken away from her with immediate effect and she should be forbidden to instruct other riders. Pester knew that horses and riding were Sara's life. Taking them away from her would be like taking her life itself away. So she put everything she had into succeeding in her aim, and she was by now well on her way. She used every conceivable contact to reach the 'heart' of the Riding Federation—the Disciplinary Board.

She helped Veronica and some other people to write accusations. Everyone who had any kind of aversion to Sara was contacted. They were encouraged by Pester to write to the Disciplinary Board and notify them of any sin they considered Sara had committed. 'Let your imagination flow,' as she put it. It was important to get as much material as possible sent in, and as quickly as possible, so that the Disciplinary Board could really understand how bad things were. What's more she had managed to get Bud Mudie on board in her official challenge to people to report Sara.

Sara's friends realized the danger and they too wrote letters to the Disciplinary Board, all in the hope of being able to tell them how things really were and how terribly wrong the undeserved attacks on Sara were.

Never before had the Disciplinary Board been so over-whelmed with letters. Half the writers claimed that Sara was an animal abuser of a kind rarely seen before. The other half asserted that they had never in any circumstances seen her treat a horse badly.

Two months went by. Sara had still not found out what she was accused of. The only things she knew were what Pester wrote in the paper. According to her Sara had been reported by Veronica, Steve's groom and two riding instructors at the Riding Club. The articles didn't give away what these reports contained but Pester led her readers to believe that they were incredibly serious charges.

Finally Sara was told in a brief letter from the Disciplinary Board that they intended to visit the Riding Club. They would question both her and her accusers. Sara welcomed that decision with great satisfaction. Finally she would have the chance to defend herself. If the Board also questioned her accusers, they would soon find out that they had had help in writing their 'witness statements'. She was also pleased that they would then see Mozart as well. Then all the accusations would fall by their own absurdity.

Time passed. Every day Sara was expecting to hear when the visit would take place. After about a week she couldn't stand it any longer. She rang up the Board. She was told that the Board first had to have a meeting and that she would be allowed to see all the letters which had been received. They would be posted directly after the meeting. She could ring John Meadow after the next weekend to find out when they would be coming. She waited for the rest of the week to finally find out something.

'John Meadow.' Sara introduced herself and told him that

she had been told that she could ring him. 'So will all the letters which have come in be sent to me by post today then?' She tried to sound as unconcerned as possible, although she felt terribly ill-at-ease talking to him.

He didn't sound particularly friendly when he replied, 'No, they won't. I can't post them.'

'Can't you post them?'

'No, I don't have your address.'

'Don't you have my address?' She was so amazed that she couldn't help sounding like a parrot. Meadow continued, if possible even more irritably: 'You have written page after page in your defence, but you didn't have the energy to write your address.'

Sara tried to avoid showing how much his words hurt her. 'But surely the Riding Federation must have my address anyway, both on the Register and on all my papers.'

'I actually do have other things to do apart from running around looking for your address.' Now he was really curt. Sara realized that it was best to pretend she hadn't noticed it. She asked him to take down her address, so perhaps he would be so kind as to send them the next day? 'I would really like to know what I am accused of and have a chance to respond to the accusations.' She put on her most friendly tone of voice in order not to antagonize him unnecessarily.

'I'll see if I have time.' He was not even trying to sound friendly. Sara continued by asking when they intended coming to the Riding School. 'I don't know. It's not at all certain that we shall come.'

Sara couldn't understand that. If they didn't come how would they find out how things really were? 'We can do that anyway.' That was the end of the conversation. Sara was left sitting there with the receiver in her hand.

A few days later an enormous envelope arrived from the Disciplinary Board. Sara opened it with shaking hands. She read. One letter after the other spoke of how obnoxious she was. How she ill treated the horses she rode. The fact that she caused accidents when the riding school horses heard how her horse was suffering.

Sara couldn't believe it was true. If the Board had read this then they must have realized what level it was. 'The horses had heard'. . .? She read it again. It was so crazy that she thought she was dreaming. So that was why the Board had decided not to come and Meadow said that they could make a decision anyway. Now she understood. If anyone had read these letters, they didn't need to talk to the people who had written them.

One of the 'witness statements' came from one of the riding instructors. She described in detail how she had witnessed when Sara rode a stallion one time. She even remembered the date, the ninth of January. She had observed how Sara ill treated a poor stallion, as she had put it, it was like a 'terrible demonstration of the art of breaking down a horse'.

Sara took out her diary which she wrote up every day. She flicked through the pages. The ninth of January? The only stallion she had ridden, and which had been difficult, was the one she had had a few months earlier. But that had not been until the end of January, for sure. On the ninth of January she'd ridden no stallion at all. She knew that now and she thanked her lucky stars that she always kept a diary of everything she did. She wondered why this riding instructor had waited so long before reporting something she'd been so upset by.

At the time, when she'd been riding the stallion, nobody had said anything. But now, many months later, people suddenly knew exactly how and when the 'animal abuse' had been perpetrated, as they put it.

Moreover, Susy Sanders, Steve's groom, had put in an almost identical report. The fact that they seemed to be written on the same typewriter and were dated the same day, reinforced Sara's suspicions that the campaign was being coordinated.

She read: 'I hope you realize what damage Sara has done to our great riding club. It would be hard to find a worse model. She has behaved equally cruelly towards the police horses as she has to all the other horses she has ridden. In the police they are glad to be rid of her and we don't want her in our club either.' The letter continued in the same vein. Sara realized what an incredible effort was being put into driving her out of the arena. Not just out of the riding club arena but out of the police arena too.

Veronica's letter was very long. Together with Mike Jacobi, the other riding instructor, she had described in detail how important it was to bar Sara from riding as quickly as possible. The fact that Sara couldn't see this herself was just further proof of her guilt! They had already written to the Riding Federation after Pester's first articles. But then, in spite of their indignation, they had not been able to cite any specific incident. Now, after Bud Mudie's and Eve Pester's challenge in the paper to report Sara, they had suddenly remembered an incident.

In two identical reports they described in detail how Sara 'on the same day as Eve Pester had called her, had taken out her poor horse and ill treated it'. They said that the reason was that Sara had been so angry after that conversation with Pester. She had whipped it, pulled on the reins to saw at its mouth and jabbed it with her spurs. The poor horse had been completely annihilated afterwards. These two reports were most probably written on the same typewriter too, and were dated the same day as the other two.

Sara shook her head. She couldn't even take it in, it was so crazy. She read the next letter. It was signed by Ken Lehman and dated the same day as the others. Together with eight school riders he claimed to have been a witness when Sara had ill treated Joo Bergman's horse on the third of April. Sara picked up her diary again. Third of April? She wasn't in the stable at all that day. She had had a clinic in a different town! This was completely mad! How could Ken Lehman sign that he and eight other people had seen Sara ill treat a horse when she hadn't even been there?

She began to doubt her own sanity. Was she the one who was mad? She rang Joo. Did she know whether Sara had ridden her horse at all on the third of April? And if so did she have the impression that she had ill treated it? Joo confirmed what Sara already knew. Sara hadn't ridden the horse on the third of April. 'Surely that was when you had a clinic wasn't it? That's what I've written in my diary anyway.' The voice at the other end of the line was agitated. 'Is someone saying that you not only rode my horse that day but also that you ill treated it? It was in a stable several miles away and you were in another town!' Joo thought the whole thing was so dreadful that Sara didn't even need to worry about how the Disciplinary Board would view the allegations.

Sara put the phone down. She read Ken's letter again. How in the world could he claim that eight other people had seen something which couldn't even have happened? Admittedly the other eight hadn't signed the letter but how dare he claim something like that?

When Sara had read all the letters she was more angry than sorry. They were all so absurd and full of preposterous and unreasonable hatred, that they should have been thrown straight into the waste paper basket.

Sara looked in the envelope. She couldn't find all the letters which she knew had reached the Riding Federation from her friends. Jenny had written. Joo and Bob had written. Not to mention Dave, Rose and Bill. They were just a few of the ones she knew had reacted and written. She also knew that there had been a meeting in the stable at the Riding Club among all the private horse owners. They had shown her the letter they had agreed to write. Sara remembered how happy she had been when she read it. They had claimed that although Sara rode every day, they had never ever seen her treat any horse in a disturbing way. On the contrary, they admired her way of handling horses. They thought it was incredibly tragic that she had been exposed to this hate campaign. Why were none of those letters there?

Sara pulled herself together and dialled John Meadow's number. Why hadn't they questioned the accusers and why weren't the letters from her friends in the envelope with the others? She also wanted to know what she was expected to do now that she had finally found out what the accusations were. When he answered she told him what was on her mind. Meadow couldn't understand what she was talking about at all, when she asked about the other letters, the ones which spoke to her credit. 'They have nothing to do with this at all. I've sorted them out and put them in a separate pile. There's nothing in them about you ill treating the horses!' He sounded surprised. Sara was amazed at his reply. 'But they must be given as much weight as the letters which accuse me surely?' He was silent for a long moment before he replied, 'I hadn't thought of that.'

Sara abandoned that subject and went on with her questions. Why hadn't they questioned her accusers? 'They weren't the ones who had done anything and needed to be questioned, if anything you're the one who should be questioned.'

Sara felt herself losing her grip more and more as the conversation went on. Finally she asked what she was expected to do now. 'Nothing. You'll be told our decision.'

21

The abyss

Spring had come and gone without Sara noticing. Summer had come but she was walking around as if in a trance. Things were getting seriously tight with money, since she didn't have any pupils any more. Even if she had had, she was banned by the Riding Club from running any training there.

She didn't even have the income from her monthly column in the horse journal. After Pester's first article Sara had rung the editor in chief and talked to her. At that point there had been no problem; Sara had been given the impression that the woman had every understanding for her situation. 'Don't worry, it'll work out, you'll see,' she had said. But in the next issue Sara's column had been cut. The editor was unavailable.

The competition season with Mozart came to nought and Sara was in a state which can only be called chaotic. Pester hadn't written any articles for a few weeks. Sara was lulled into a false sense of security—perhaps the public attacks were over.

She was sitting looking at the daily paper somewhat distractedly. A headline leapt out at her: 'DRESSAGE RIDER TO BE DISCIPLINED AFTER MIDSUMMER.' Pester was able to report that the Disciplinary Board had decided to come to the Riding Club to decide Sara's fate—probably to order a long and serious ban from everything to do with horses. In view of the serious reports which had reached the Riding Federation after the revelations in the paper about Sara's cruelty to animals, there was no question of her being allowed to work with horses.

Sara's soul, which was already severely wounded, was totally unprepared for Pester's new attack. It was just too much. Once again she fell into the black abyss. The last thing she remembers is spiralling down into a black hole.

She's back.

She is so cold she's shivering, but she's too weak to do anything about it. She is lying on her bunk—the only thing still keeping her alive is hope; the hope which she has carried within her ever since the day she was pushed down the stairs and carried off.

She has seen her mother and her sister leave their life on this earth, and she feels many years older than she actually is. She can't cry any more. Her tears have dried up a long time ago, but she knows that if she can just hold out a little longer, she will see her father again. He will come and fetch her, she knows it. If only she can hold out.

'I'm so cold.' The words are almost inaudible as she whispers them, but suddenly she feels somebody tugging at her. 'So you're cold are you? Well then we'll have to make sure you get warm.' The voice which she heard from far, far away was icy cold and unfamiliar to her. The next moment she feels a heat which is unreal and incomprehensible. The flames silence her last despairing scream.

She lay huddled in the foetal position on the floor when she came to again. Her body was shaking uncontrollably and her heart was pounding. She tried to persuade herself to calm down. She felt that if she succumbed to the terror, that would be the end of her. She concentrated hard and tried to breathe more slowly.

Gradually she felt that she was beginning to regain control; her heart was not pounding so hard any more and her breathing was calmer. She knew that she had relived her own death. She had experienced how she had been robbed of life in her previous existence.

How was it possible for this to happen? There was nobody, nobody at all, she could talk to. Who would understand? She didn't even understand herself what was happening to her. What was required of her for her soul to be free and released from the straitjacket which had bound her for so long? What had she done to deserve this hell? Had she herself in some other life been so evil that she was now compelled to go through this?

No, God in heaven, let it not be so. Sara folded her hands together and prayed from the depths of her soul: 'Oh God, dear God, I pray you, open a door to me so that I can see the meaning of what is happening to me. Show me how I can be freed from my memories and my tormentors. Both from the past and the present. Help me, dear Father, help me …' During her prayer she fell into a deep sleep. She slept calmly for the first time in a long while.

'How can they make a decision when they haven't even spoken to me at all?' The words were Sara's. She was putting the question to one of the representatives of the Riding Federation. He had just informed her that a decision had been made on her 'case'. He couldn't say more. Dejectedly Sara put down the receiver.

Alec Peterson had written to the Disciplinary Board some weeks earlier and tried to arrange to meet with them, but in vain. So now they had made a decision, without giving her the least chance to say anything about the so-called charges. 'Can you understand how they can have made a decision without at least talking to me first?' Sara put the question to Alec. He tried to calm her down. He agreed that it was a strange way of going about things. They should have asked her to respond to the individual charges. From their actions he concluded that they must have written off the whole thing and acquitted Sara. Surely they must have finally realized how crazy it all was? 'What's more,' said Alec, in an attempt to calm Sara down, 'you don't need to be at all worried. If, against all expectations, they have still believed the charges, they can't actually do anything. It isn't a punishable offence to treat your horse the way they say you have. Steve admitted it and was acquitted! What's more you weren't even riding on two of the occasions which were reported.'

In fact this was true. But Sara knew that she would never live it down if they ruled that she had been cruel to horses. Regardless of whether they could punish her or not. Surely they couldn't do things this way? Or could they? Sara didn't know. The only thing she knew for sure was that the whole thing had been very well prepared, everything that had happened and was still happening.

And then the Disciplinary Board decision came through. It basically said that they had not been able to make any decision. Since what she had done had occurred in training and not in competitions, they couldn't give a ruling. The regulations didn't cover incidents which occurred during training. The competition regulations were only for competitions. Those regulations stipulated very precisely what applied, but apart from that, according to the Disciplinary Board, there were no rules governing how a horse should be treated. Against that background they had dropped the case.

Sara read this and tried to understand it. But no matter how many times she read it, she was none the wiser. How could the Riding Federation and the Disciplinary Board read these accusations and then not bother to investigate them?

If the charges had really been true, the Board's 'decision' meant that they didn't care at all whether horses were ill-treated as long as it didn't happen during a competition! And it was just as bad if the accusations were untrue. The Board didn't care that an innocent person was being pilloried for cruelty to animals without any chance of a fair hearing. Indeed one might well ask why on earth the Board existed at all?

Was this cowardice due to the fact that they didn't dare oppose Pester and her newspaper? Was it easier to refrain from conducting an investigation, with the risk of being obliged to admit that all the accusations were cooked up lies, if that would have meant that they had to openly accuse Pester of peddling untruths?

The more she thought about it, the angrier she got. She realized that if she was ever to be cleared of these accusations, she would be forced to take on the whole Establishment. But with the rage she felt inside at being treated in this despicable way, she would never give up. It might cost her money and strength, but she must at all costs continue her battle for justice and redress. Regardless of how long it took and what she would be obliged to go through.

Alec Peterson was absolutely furious when he rang Sara: 'We must appeal against this, I've never seen anything so horrendous.' He was so upset that his voice was almost cracking. Sara was pleased that his reaction was so strong and that she was not the only one to think that this was a cowardly and infamous injustice against her. More than once Sara had offered Bob a silent thank you in her thoughts for putting her in touch with Alec. He was dependability personified and her lifeline when everything was collapsing around her.

The day after the 'decision' was announced, Pester had another full page in the paper. This was the twelfth article about Sara from her pen. When she opened the paper Sara was confronted with a picture of Veronica and Mike. Above it stood in bold type: 'NEITHER ACQUITTED NOR CONVICTED.'

In the article Veronica was quoted as saying, 'I am both angry and disappointed, but naturally I'm going to appeal. You can't just accept horses being treated like this. This person must quite simply get out of the sport.' Bud Mudie was also quoted: 'The rules must be revised if this sort of thing can go on without the rider in question being punished.' He also said how important it was to appeal against the decision.

The media attention was once again overwhelming. They talked about it on the radio news. Sara was interviewed, not to get her view on the matter but simply to answer the reporter's questions. 'You have been accused of sawing at the horses' mouths. Did you use a saw?'

Sara didn't know what to say. Her throat was choked with tears and she was battling not to let it show. She pulled herself together. 'First of all I haven't ever sawed at any horse's mouth and secondly this is an expression in riding terminology which means pulling the bit backwards and forwards in the horse's mouth. Naturally it has nothing to do with a saw!'

Now truth really is much much stranger than fiction, she thought to herself, when the reporter looked at her with disappointment. He didn't seem at all convinced that she was telling the truth. But in the radio broadcast that question and answer were left out.

Another reporter rang from the biggest riding journal in Sweden. She had previously written several articles about Sara's alleged acts of cruelty, all in the same vein as Pester and without asking Sara's views on the matter. But now she wanted her comments. Her tone was very sharp even as she introduced herself: 'What do you think about the judgment? You are neither acquitted nor convicted.'

Sara said she was shocked that the people on the Board had had a meeting about her without even allowing her to speak for herself. She would have appreciated having a chance to respond to the allegations. Then she could have told them that she had not even been present on two of the occasions of alleged ill-treatment.

'Of course you have had a chance to respond to the charges. The Disciplinary Board has been out and questioned you! You had nothing to say, the evidence against you was over-whelming!' She didn't try to conceal her triumph.

Sara couldn't believe she had heard correctly. The Board was supposed to have been out and questioned her? 'But nobody has been here. I have not been interviewed. And what's this evidence you're talking about? I'm the one who can prove that I'm innocent. If only I was given the chance!'

Now the reporter got really mad. She accused Sara of being a liar and a coward. 'Don't lie through your teeth to me. I know they were there!' Now she was screaming in Sara's ear and she had to hold the receiver away from her. It was absolutely pointless trying to talk to her, Sara realized, so she said nothing. The reporter concluded the conversation: 'I know what sort of a person you are. Both you and your boss, who you lived with, got kicked out of the police. They don't do that for no reason!'

The phone was slammed down. Anger and helplessness flooded over Sara in that moment. She crashed the receiver down so that the telephone fell to the floor with a bang. She seldom swore but now a stream of oaths came pouring out till she almost embarrassed herself.

The next day Pester continued her unrelenting work. She had by now written about fifteen articles and was very pleased with the results. She had also contacted the man who was behind the sponsorship project with Mozart. And the outcome wasn't slow in coming. The man rang Sara and told her that he was not interested in her having Mozart any longer. He didn't want her in his sponsorship scheme any longer. Not because he believed that she had hit her horse. On the contrary he had been to the Riding Club many times, even when Sara was unaware of it, and he had watched her riding. It had always looked good he thought. But it was no use. He didn't think there was any point any more with all this negative publicity about Sara and the horse.

Sara tried to get him to understand that she didn't think it was good either, but that she really needed all the support she could get. Especially as he knew that they were all lies which were being spread about and nothing else. She didn't know what she would do if Mozart was taken away from her. But the man was absolutely cold. Sara couldn't believe that he was the same man who had rung her up and talked so warmly and kindly to try and persuade her to find a suitable horse. He simply replied that it was not his problem if she didn't know what to do. She tried desperately to get him to change his mind but in vain. He had decided, he didn't want anything to do with Sara any more. He would deal with the arrangements as soon as possible and that was the end of the conversation.

Once again it felt as if the skies were falling in on Sara. If they took her horse away from her, then they had won. What would she do? She tried to think clearly. Two thirds of the horse didn't belong to her. The sponsor owned one third and the Riding Federation one third. What would they say if she wanted to buy their shares? She had no idea whether it was financially viable for her but it was the only solution, as far as she could see.

After a few days, when the Riding Federation rang her up and told her that Mozart was to be sold, Sara heard herself say that she wanted to buy him. First there was a deathly silence and then she was told that they couldn't give her an answer immediately. They would discuss it in the Federation and then she would be told. When she put down the receiver she felt herself shaking. What had she said? Buy Mozart? How would she manage it?

She loved her horse and the mere thought that he might be taken from her was unbearable. Money! She must raise the money somehow. If they agreed to let her buy the horse, she would have to be able to pay immediately, before they had time to change their minds. The only way she could think of was taking out a mortgage on the house. It wasn't very clever but she had no other choice.

'We've decided that you can buy Mozart.' Sara could breathe again. The mortgage was authorized and Mozart was hers.

22

Justice?

A month later the Appeals Board gave its ruling: 'Give a judgment on the issue and investigate to what extent the accusations are true or not,' they wrote to the Disciplinary Board. All the members resigned. The Riding Federation hastened to appoint a new board. A board which would 'have the guts to get tough' as Bud Mudie expressed it. Pester was delighted in her next article.

History now repeated itself: Sara received a large envelope—three times as thick as the previous one—from the new Disciplinary Board. She was pleased. Obviously they had also sent the letters which spoke for her this time. But when she opened the envelope she discovered that this was not the case at all. The reason there was so much paper was that they had sent two copies, sometimes even three, of every letter which had come in. Didn't they have enough with what there was? Did they have to do this to make it look more than it was? Sara couldn't understand.

She also got a letter from the Board's new secretary. Sara jumped when she saw the signature and felt terribly uneasy. Paul Vermont was a previous member of the Riding Club Board. He was one of the people who had appointed Cyle and Veronica. Now he was a member of a board which was to judge whether Sara was guilty of cruelty to animals or not.

In the letter he asked for answers to various questions, among other things what she had to say about the accusation against her relating to the ninth of January when it was claimed that she had ill-treated a stallion. The accuser had now realized that it was a different day, namely the seventh of January. Sara checked her diary again and confirmed that she hadn't ridden the stallion until the end of January. On the seventh she had been to the hospital with her mother for a check-up. She hadn't been in the stables that day at all.

She read on in Paul Vermont's letter: 'You are also asked to respond to the accusations about Mozart and Amadeus.' Did they think they were two different horses? Sara was horrified when she realized how little they really knew. And they would decide her whole future! She was to be put 'on trial' by a Board who didn't even know how many horses they were talking about, who didn't care that the accuser had changed the date to try and find a day when she had at least been riding. Maybe they wouldn't care either whether Sara could prove that she hadn't even been in the stable at the time of the 'crime'. And yet now she was supposed to respond and explain herself.

She had an awful premonition that this new board had been appointed for one purpose only: to ensure that she was 'hanged' and thus save the skin of both the Riding Federation and the Disciplinary Board. All for the sake of placating Eve Pester and getting her to shut up and calm down.

Alec wrote a fresh application to the Disciplinary Board. He listed all the discrepancies in detail. After a certain amount of detective work, he was also able to tell them the truth about Veronica, and that it perhaps was no accident that she had been in the Riding Club when the financial irregularities were discovered. Her criminal 'escapades' in the financial field had meant that she had been on the police wanted list for some time, suspected of serious fraud and document forgery. Alec also reminded the Board of Sara's persistent attempts to draw the attention of the Club's managers to the shortfalls in the till. And that was not all. After the Riding Manager had had to resign from office and Veronica had put all the blame on him, he had not wanted to go on living. A few months later he had taken his own life.

Veronica had also had to leave the Club after the new managers had examined the accounts. But she was so clever in what she did that it was impossible to trace where the money had gone. What is more she had been free to do as she pleased since Sara had been fully occupied in defending herself against all the attacks by Pester.

Even though the managers had recognized that Veronica had feathered her own nest, nobody could prove anything. So she had been dismissed officially on the grounds of poor work. The fact that nobody in the management wanted to start digging into her finances might also have had something to do with the way Veronica promised loud and long that anyone who argued with her would have their own accounts soundly scrutinized by a journalist called Pester. Some of the directors had their own businesses and for some reason they were not keen on having a journalist start digging into their affairs.

Veronica was now helping Mike in his new business, which he ran together with his sister. Sara knew that neither Mike nor his sister had any idea of Veronica's background and that they would be easy prey for her. Sooner or later their eyes would be opened.

Alec also pointed out to the Board that there was a vet's certificate which Sara had sent in immediately after the Easter weekend, but which had never been mentioned. Now he was also sending a statement which Lou Fleming had written out. She was the one who had ridden Sara's horse the day after the alleged incident, so she should have noticed whether the horse was injured in any way. Lou's letter said that she had not seen anything unusual whatsoever in Mozart. There was nothing to suggest that the allegation was true according to her.

'There were no witnesses present when you rode Mozart that day you spoke to Pester, were there? The day before the first article?' Alec tried to get Sara to remember. But Sara didn't remember that she had been with Rita and Steve. So much had happened these last few months that she had forgotten. Or else she had subconsciously suppressed some things, quite simply in order to survive. Be that as it may, it was completely wiped from Sara's memory, so she had to disappoint Alec. 'No, I think I was alone.'

'Your word against theirs. But with the vet's certificate, Lou's statement and the proof that the other allegations are untrue, the Board must realize that all in all Veronica's and Mike's allegation falls by its own absurdity too. What's more it's not up to you to prove your innocence. It's the accusers who bear the burden of proof. And there's absolutely nothing they can say.' Alec was full of confidence. The stallion's owner and Joo had both given written statements that their horses were neither ill-treated nor ridden by Sara on the days in question. They also attested that Sara had not treated their horses in the way she was accused of on any other day either.

'There are some lawyers on this Board after all, and naturally they know what the laws of the land are. So you needn't be a bit worried, everything will work out, you'll see.' Alec's calm voice and conviction were like balm to Sara's restless soul. It was six months since the witch hunt had begun. Half a year robbed from Sara's life. She no longer had the inner strength she had always had before in her life to rely on. The nightmares day and night had haunted her for six months. She was completely drained, body and soul.

The people who had determined to eliminate the risk of her appealing to the Equal Opportunities Board or stop her from questioning where the money was going, had won. The persecution had been, and still was, so enormous and well-planned that Sara could barely manage to survive each day.

The new Disciplinary Board had its first meeting about Sara a few months later. She harboured a certain faint hope that they might decide to come and talk to her. And perhaps take a look at Mozart? The day after the meeting came a press release. The Board had reached a decision, to be announced one month later. 'One month later?' Sara hardly had the energy to react at all, but Alec hit the roof! 'Do you know why they need a month's grace?' Sara wondered whether Alec knew. 'You won't believe this,' he replied, 'but the Board's secretary has to have his holiday first!'

He was right, Sara couldn't believe it was true. It was a long month. During that time Pester and some of her colleagues kept the pot boiling. Every so often announcements and articles, great and small, were published.

One month later the decision was announced. Sara received it through the letter-box. In spite of everything she wasn't nervous. Deep down inside she still believed in justice and the idea that the people on the Board were sane, sensible people who knew the law. She therefore felt relatively calm as she opened the envelope.

23

'Guilty'

'The Disciplinary Board has received a number of letters and reports from staff at the Riding Club, with information that while training horses Sara Carpenter repeatedly subjected the horses to heavy-handed treatment by pulling strongly on their mouths and heavy use of spurs and by hitting them with her stick. It has also been claimed that she has been riding like this for several years, which has caused feelings to run very high.

'The Board has also received letters from various people, among others elite riders and owners of horses which the rider has trained, who have expressed admiration for her and her riding. These people have stated that they have never seen her ill-treat a horse. They have claimed that she has been the subject of victimization.

'The Board can therefore record that there are differing opinions about Sara Carpenter's riding in general. However one should not conclude from this that the people who are critical and have reported her have spoken out against their better judgement nor that their information might be an expression of the victimization of an individual.'

Sara read and read. She refused to comprehend. They didn't believe her. They believed more in Veronica and the riding instructors. 'There is no reason to question the information which the accusers have submitted.' She could scarcely continue reading. 'The Disciplinary Board considers it reliably proven that Sara Carpenter has been guilty of what she is

accused of and the Board therefore hereby orders that she be reprimanded.'

Everything went black before Sara's eyes. They had condemned her for something she could demonstrably not have done. She wasn't even there. 'There was no reason to question...?' 'Reliably proven.' What did they mean by that? Nothing had been investigated, much less proven.

For the first time in her life Sara felt doubt—perhaps it wasn't true that Good always conquered. Was she now beaten?

There was no doubt now that her chances of writing to the Equal Opportunities Board about the post of chief officer of the Mounted Police had been blown away. It would never be possible to repair the damage to her credibility. Regardless of whether she ever got redress, it would be too late.

Veronica had also succeeded. Sara hadn't spared a thought for her or the Club's finances after Pester's first call. But hadn't Pester also won? She had now put an end to Sara and her riding—once and for all?

Would Sara have the drive to continue her battle for redress and justice? In her heart she knew the answer to that question before she had even asked it. It was a battle not only for the person she was now, but also for the one she had been and for the one she would become. It was not just the previous life which was connected to this one. The next life would also be affected to the utmost degree by what happened in this one.

Sara knew that. And even though she felt like David before Goliath, she felt that she was forced, once and for all, to dare to confront her persecutors, no matter what. She could challenge them in this life. She hadn't been able to do that in her previous one. Then she had been a defenceless victim of evil, together with millions of other people. Now it was just her own courage, and her free will, which would decide her future.

When she had come to herself a little, she rang Alec. He was shocked, angry and appalled. But he promised her that if she had the heart to continue he would never give up. 'This is the worst miscarriage of justice I have ever seen in my thirty years in this profession. It is a total meltdown in legal terms.' Alec had a certain way with words, being the lawyer he was. They agreed that Alec should write a fresh letter to the Appeals Board and demand that the highest sports authority in Sweden, the Sports Council, should be allowed to judge 'the case'. He was convinced that they would turn the Riding Federation and the Disciplinary Board upside down when they learned of the ruling and the reasons why Sara had been given a reprimand.

The next day Pester was able to celebrate her victory. There was a whole page in the paper with Sara in her police uniform on her horse and the headline 'CONVICTED' in large letters. Pester had chosen the photo very carefully. In the picture Sara was raising her right hand. To the uninitiated it might look as though she was doing it to hit the horse she was sitting on. The photo had been taken several years earlier, when Sara was still working as a mounted police officer. It had been taken for a journal doing a feature on signs for horse traffic. The sign Sara was making on the photo showed what to do if you wanted drivers to slow down—you move your right arm up and down with the palm downwards.

In the text Pester gave free rein to her delight at Sara's misfortune. She said what an incredible victory it was for all the horses in the country and naturally mentioned that it was thanks to her that a delinquent like Sara had now been stopped. It was Pester who had exposed Sara, now the 'ex' mounted police officer. It needed no stretch of the imagination for the readers to believe that Sara had been dismissed thanks to Pester.

Sara thought she would be sick as she read the article. Even though she had been absolutely certain the day before that she would never give up her battle, she didn't feel so confident any more. And then when the riding journals took up the story as well—even the one which Sara had previously written for, and expressed their delight that she had 'finally been convicted on the evidence of her guilt and that it was a good thing Pester had been able to expose her', she felt that her very existence was threatened. She wondered how she would find the strength to go on living another day in this nightmare.

But the days passed and Sara survived. Not least because her mother, like a gift from above, was finally allowed home from hospital and, what's more, stronger than she had been for a long time.

When Sara read Alec's letter to the Appeals Board, it was absolutely obvious how desperately absurd the whole thing was. Alec had divided it into sections in an easily understood way, point by point, so that nothing could be misunderstood. Sara's hope that it must be possible to set this folly right, sooner or later, was renewed.

They are like a pack of wild wolves, thought Sara, one starts chasing a quarry and the others follow on behind. The leading wolf howls and the others join in. When they catch up with their appointed prey they tear it to pieces among themselves without even looking at what it is they have thrown themselves upon.

The Appeals Board took a long time to reply, but finally gave a ruling that the Sports Council should judge the case. They also enclosed a letter which had been sent to them by Veronica

List and Mike Jacobi. Sara was asked to submit her views on their claims. The submission from Veronica and Mike was forty-four pages long. Every page, every line, was concocted from the most fantastic lies. How could she respond to that?

Sara sat down and tried. After a while she put down her pen. She couldn't. She felt like an idiot when she realized that she had written that the grazes on Mozart's hind legs were due to his lying in his box at night and that it was not she, Sara, who had caused them. The vet had noted that Mozart's skin was a little rubbed and Veronica and Mike had picked up on that. Naturally it was Sara who had beaten the horse sore!

Sara was even more annoyed with herself when she realized that she had tried to explain that the vet did not usually ride the horses he examined. 'The horse is mentally broken down, not physically,' as Veronica had expressed it. She confidently asserted that a vet must of course ride a horse which he examines.

The fact that Lou Fleming, the most competent dressage rider in Sweden, had ridden Mozart the day after Sara was supposed to have beaten him half to death, and what is more had provided a written statement to the effect that she had seen nothing wrong, was dismissed lightly by Veronica: the reason Lou had not realized that the horse was a complete wreck was because Lou was such a good rider. In her hands Mozart was naturally both calm and sweet-tempered!

Sara realized that it was impossible to respond to this kind of thing; it was quite simply beneath her dignity even to try. If the Sports Council couldn't see that Veronica and Mike were completely 'away with the fairies' well then there was nothing she could say to convince them.

Sara read on in their submission. Suddenly a few lines caught her eye: 'What's more, Sara was not riding alone in the school on that day, but Steve Meyer was also there and another rider whose name we can't remember.' Sara read it several times. She had thought that she had been alone in the indoor school for that short time that she had ridden Mozart after Pester's first telephone call. She only knew that she had been so terribly upset by what was happening and had thought that she was alone when she had walked her horse for a little while. But now suddenly Veronica and Mike said that this was not the case at all.

Sara pounced on the phone and rang Steve. 'Yes, it was the same day that we were both called by Eve Pester. After the call we rode together, that's right.' Steve was absolutely sure. Now the memories were coming back to Sara as well. She had come into the ring and Rita Johnson was already there. Moments later Steve had also come in and all three had ridden round and talked about Pester's call. Rita had comforted her.

Sara couldn't understand how she could have forgotten that. Before Steve hung up, he asked Sara why she hadn't confessed like he had. 'There was no problem at all, Veronica helped me to write my apology, she was really helpful. And Pester said she wasn't really after me at all.'

Sara couldn't believe her ears. Had Veronica helped Steve to write his apology? And Pester hadn't been 'after Steve'!

It was becoming increasingly clear to Sara what was actually going on. She didn't have the heart to answer Steve's question, she just thanked him. She felt relieved in spite of everything, not so much because Steve could confirm that she was telling the truth but also because she had realized that Rita had also been riding at the same time.

Naturally they could make a lot out of it if she took Steve as a witness: 'Now one horse abuser is supporting the other . . .' Sara could see Pester's headline before her eyes. But Rita was a trained riding instructor and had long experience of horses and riding; you couldn't just dismiss her or challenge her evidence. Sara fumbled and could hardly dial the number, she was so anxious to contact Rita. 'Yes, I remember it very well. We rode round and talked about Pester's call, you and I and Steve.' Rita didn't hesitate a moment. 'Are they claiming that something happened then?' Rita sounded surprised. 'Do you remember seeing me hit my horse?' Sara had to put a straight question. 'But of course you didn't. This is all so ridiculous that surely there must be an end to it soon? Are they out of their minds?' Now Rita didn't sound surprised any more, just angry.

Sara put the receiver down, liberated. Now finally there was an end to the nightmare. She had two witnesses who both could and would attest that she had spoken the truth the whole time. She rang Alec's number, at the same time as she thanked the Force which had ensured that Veronica and Mike had unwittingly helped her.

If Sara had told Alec that he had won a million crowns, he couldn't have been happier. 'So we'll ask them to write a couple of lines to the Sports Council and that'll be the end of it. It won't be easy for the Riding Federation and the Disciplinary Board when this gets out. If they had just carried out a proper investigation from the start, they could have saved you a lot of unnecessary suffering.' Alec was enormously upset about the way Sara had been treated, and he intended to spare no effort in making sure that those responsible should be held to account as soon as Sara was cleared.

The letters from Rita and Steve were sent to the Sports Council. They declared that they had seen Sara riding on the day in question and that there had been no heavy-handedness at all. The claims of ill-treatment were pure lies they said.

Sara could breathe again. Now, on top of all the other evidence, there were two witnesses to testify that she was telling the truth and that Mike and Veronica were lying. 'Now you can rest assured. They just can't get out of this without acquitting you completely of all the charges. You don't need even to try and respond to Veronica and Mike's accusations. Nothing can change the fact that you have two witnesses and they have none.'

Alec was very pleased. He knew, and had always known, that Sara was telling the truth. But it still felt good to him to have it confirmed. And it made him if anything even more determined to pin down the 'incompetents' on the various boards. Not to mention the Riding Federation, which had thrown Sara to the wolves without giving it a second thought. Just to save their own skins.

In Alec's eyes they were pretty useless. For them to be members of an organization which among other things was supposed to safeguard the riders' interests was a mockery, he thought. It was his confirmed opinion that they took care of their own interests and nobody else's.

Another two months went by. Rita told Sara that a member of the Sports Council had phoned her and that she had also given her statement to him verbally.

Sara was looking forward to their decision happily and confidently. Finally she would be vindicated.

24

Guilty–not guilty

The decision had been made and would be announced in a week. Sara was somewhat concerned. Why should it take a week if they had made the decision? 'You've no need to worry at all. They probably need the time to formulate it in such a way that nobody can criticize them when they clear you completely. They know the press is hot on the trail of this one.' Alec was full of reassurance. He lived in the belief that justice was something you could take for granted.

It was a long week and Sara became more and more impatient. The last night before the decision was to be announced, she didn't sleep a wink. 'Just imagine if her persecutors had somehow managed to get at the Sports Council itself? Imagine if they just dismissed Rita and Steve's evidence? Imagine if...?'

At twelve o'clock the next day the decision was to be made public. Three minutes after twelve Alec rang. 'They've set aside the Disciplinary Board's ruling, you won't get a reprimand, but...' Sara could tell that something was not quite right.

Alec's voice was strained and somewhat subdued. 'Well, it's very odd. They have written in their ruling that they can't discipline you since the Riding Federation's regulations don't cover what happens during training. They have concluded that you haven't damaged the reputation of the sport, since only a small circle of people have seen what you've done.'

'Have seen what I've done?' Sara sat down, she felt that her legs wouldn't support her any longer.

'I really can't understand it at all,' continued Alec unhappily. 'They note that you are guilty of what you are accused of, but that they can't punish you for it. They haven't taken any notice at all of our witnesses and simply confirm that the accusers are telling the truth.'

Sara heard Alec's rueful voice further and further away. She was losing her grip on reality. She put down the receiver gently and got up. It all seemed unreal. She left the house in a fog. She went down to the stream which ran through her garden. Alone among the trees with the water at her feet, she sank down on to the grass. Martin found her there many hours later. He sat down silently at her side and took her hand. Neither of them said anything, they had a closeness to each other which went far beyond any words. They sat there together for a long, long time. In silence. As he had so many times before, it was Martin who renewed Sara's will to go on living. Together they went back to the warmth of the house.

Sara had to marshal all her inner reserves to go on. Was she now going to have to live out the rest of her life with the dreadful accusation unrefuted, that she was cruel to animals? How had they found her guilty but not punishable?

Pester, who had looked forward to the Sports Council putting 'the last nail in her coffin', was disappointed. Admittedly they hadn't dared to clear Sara but it was still bad enough that she wasn't going to be punished. The fact that Sara had now reached the limits of her resistance was something Pester was nonetheless convinced of, and she felt satisfaction when she thought of how her next article would push Sara a little bit closer to the edge. 'SPORTS COUNCIL FINDS SARA CARPENTER GUILTY TOO' was the headline, and the articles gave free expression to Pester's disappointment that 'a rider like this can't be punished', even though what she had done was well-known.

'But surely you're going to put all this behind you now and go forward?' The words were Andy Keller's, one of the leaders responsible for dressage in the Riding Federation. Sara had phoned him to find out how she should deal with the fact that she had been told after the Sports Council's ruling that she would be refused a trainer's licence.

Sara couldn't conceal her surprise at his question. 'How can I "put behind me" something which is destroying my life? How can I go forward and have this hanging over me as long as I live?' She couldn't understand how he could make it sound like a trifling matter.

'But we've all done it at some time, got a horse going a bit! It's just our luck that no one has seen us doing it.' He sounded almost proud of the fact that he, like everyone else, made a habit of hitting horses but had been lucky enough not to be seen.

Sara was so angry that she almost stammered when she replied: 'You must excuse me but I have actually never "got any horse going". That claim is entirely your own affair.'

What kind of double standard was this? Nobody in the Riding Federation had lifted a finger to support her and help her against Pester's attacks. Instead they had pretended to be shocked at a dressage rider using a stick and spurs in such a cruel way. Whether it was true or not didn't matter. Their attitude seemed to be that if you were stupid enough to attract such powerful enemies, you had to take the consequences. And now one of their leaders was even boasting how he, together with a lot of others, had managed not to be discovered when they'd 'got their horses going'. Sara hastened to bring the conversation to an end. She hadn't got an answer to her question about her trainer's licence.

This double standard wasn't confined to the Riding Federation. Sara realized this when she spoke to her best friend, Jenny Best. Jenny related a conversation she had had with the riding journalist who had so persistently 'howled' along with Pester. 'What would you have done if a stallion had reared up on its hind legs with you on its back?' Jenny had put the question to the journalist. 'Would you have patted it and asked it to stop?' She had really insisted on getting an answer. 'Of course you have to hit it, but you have to do it so that no one sees.' The journalist had thought it was a stupid question with an obvious answer.

Now suddenly all the wolves had gone quiet. It seemed as if they were all satisfied with the result they had achieved. Everything was fine, Sara's life was in ruins. Now she could jolly well shut up and not go harping on about that old story any longer. That seemed to be the general view.

The fact that she was branded an animal abuser was something she would have to learn to live with. The fact that her innermost being had been crushed to pieces was not their problem. The fact that she was on the brink of ruin after a year of expenses and no income was something she would kindly have to learn to accept. The fact that she was permanently barred from any higher office in her profession as a police officer was of course something else she'd just have to learn to put up with.

Her possibilities of earning her living as a dressage trainer had been eliminated and that was of course a good thing. So she couldn't pass on her so-called skills! And her books, which had always dealt with the love of animals and people, weren't particularly believable any more either. What a shame. For her.

Why should she carry on making a fuss? It would have been better if she had had the sense to confess from the start. Even if she hadn't done anything, she should have confessed. Then she would have been acquitted and everything would have blown over as quickly as it had blown up.

Or?

25

No choice

When Sara talked to Alec later, it was obvious to her that he was well and truly beside himself. After the first shock had subsided, and he had begun to think clearly again, he had decided to try and get Sara to try a new tack. He had consulted some other lawyers about the possible alternatives. Together they had worked out that the best solution would be to put the matter before a public prosecutor and try to get a public prosecution brought against the Riding Federation and the various other Boards.

The public prosecutor could undertake such a case if, as they said, it was in the public interest for a prosecution to be brought. Alec was of the very firm opinion that it must be in the public interest if the highest instance in sport discarded witnesses and vet's certificates just like that and believed absurd claims without even investigating the matter or bothering to hear the accused party in person. If it was not in the public interest to expose and challenge such goings on, then nothing was, thought Alec.

'In the present situation all sportsmen—and sportswomen—are completely without rights. Not to mention all riders. That is absolutely appalling and unacceptable.' Alec held forth eloquently to Sara, who gradually became convinced that a public prosecution might be a practicable solution. If the prosecutor were to decide to lodge a prosecution on her behalf, it wouldn't cost her anything.

Sara gave Alec the go-ahead to write to the Prosecutor's Office.

But Alec had to be paid for all the work he was doing. Even if he halved the invoices, it still meant that Sara's finances were rapidly reaching disaster level. But what choice was there? Sara felt that she had to be vindicated at any price and be cleared of all the charges. And she knew that she would never manage it without Alec.

But it would cost money to carry on, money which she didn't have and had no idea how to get. All her savings and more had gone. She had no work; she had renewed her leave of absence for a further year. It was inconceivable for her to return to the police without having set the record straight on the accusations and having her name completely cleared. She had been driven into a corner and there was only one way out—forwards.

The whole of her future would be decided by the way she now chose to act. Sara had put everything she had into taking her case this far. She knew that she would be obliged to take very drastic steps if she was to continue her fight.

But she also knew, with one hundred per cent certainty, that she couldn't go on living if she gave up hope of obtaining satisfaction. It would mean that for the rest of her life she would have to live with being branded an animal abuser. She knew that in that case she would never enjoy another carefree minute in her life. And her persecutors would have achieved what they set out to do: putting an end to her. So she had no real choice.

Her horse, Mozart, was the only thing of value Sara owned, apart from the house, which Martin, Erwin and her mother lived in with her. Selling that and uprooting the whole family was unthinkable. Selling Mozart was also unthinkable–the first few times she thought of it. Mozart, whom she loved with all her heart. Could she possibly sell him to get through the hell which had been thrust upon her? Sara was out of her mind with despair, but no matter how she revolved the problem in her mind, she could see no other solution. Mozart was the only one who could help her.

'Yes, I know lots of people interested in a horse like that, they don't just grow on trees after all!' Sara was talking to Richard Wright, a man known for dealing in horses around the world. Sara tried to sound businesslike when she talked about all Mozart's merits and his performances in the competition ring. She was constantly reminded that she was sitting there trying to sell her best friend, but she steeled herself to see the conversation through. They agreed that Richard should phone as soon as he had found a prospective buyer. Richard had been pretty keen; he could earn quite a lot of money from selling a horse like Sara's.

When she put down the phone she didn't move for some time. What had she done? How could she bear to be separated from her horse? Just imagine coming into the stable and not hearing his welcoming neigh. Never being able to ride him again. When she realized the enormity of what she was doing, it felt as though an icy hand was gripping her heart and twisting it.

Sara thought back over her life: how on many occasions she had been faced with important crossroads. Crossroads where she herself had been forced to choose her route. She had always relied on her inner voice and the Good Force. The One who always looked after her and helped her when she stumbled in the dark. She had to do that now too.

What seemed hopeless and meaningless perhaps wasn't.

There must be some meaning in everything that happened and some good had to come out of it, sooner or later. It was that belief which helped Sara to cope when Richard rang and wanted to come out with a prospective buyer.

The day before she was to show Mozart to him, a lady rang and introduced herself as Elisabet Svensson. She owned a horse which was five years old and which she wanted Sara to have and ride. 'We think the horse is great but we can't ride so I wondered whether perhaps you could consider taking him on?' Sara explained her situation and the fact that she was being obliged to sell her own horse because she needed money. So unfortunately it was impossible. 'But we are prepared to pay you for training him and pay the horse's expenses, if you think he's worth investing in for higher dressage classes.'

The woman was very anxious to persuade her. Sara couldn't believe she had heard her right. Hadn't Elisabet Svensson read the papers for the last year? Had she been on another planet? Surely nobody would want to ask Sara to take care of a horse after all that? And pay for it! Sara thought that for once she was having a pleasant dream. But it was true and they agreed that Elisabet should come over with the horse the next weekend so that Sara could see him and have a trial ride.

Sara pondered a lot about the conversation after she put the receiver down. She had asked the woman if she had read the newspapers. She had, but she didn't believe reporters for a moment, she had explained. What's more she had seen Sara on various occasions over the years in competitions. She had always thought that it looked harmonious and pleasant when Sara rode. Naturally Sara felt encouraged by the praise and the enquiry. She hoped that Magic, as the horse was called, would have potential.

He wasn't handsome—with the best will in the world you couldn't call him that. But there was something about Magic which Sara fell for straight away. Something vulnerable and fragile, which she had not found in any other horse. His eyes radiated wisdom and wonder. And his small ears pointed forward all the time. He was the total opposite of Mozart in his build—small, unmuscular and unprepossessing at first glance. His colour was brown. There were no white marks to catch the eye. He was just brown.

When Sara rode him he trotted nicely for a little while. But suddenly he just stopped as if nailed to the ground. Then suddenly, when it suited him, he trotted again. 'That's what he did with us, but he never does anything more than that.' Elisabet was worried that Sara might reject her offer when she noticed that Magic had a special will of his own.

Sara continued to ride and she felt that Magic had something about him which was very unusual. He had a really enterprising spirit and it felt as if he were very willing to work, but when he didn't understand he just stopped dead. It was just as if he was wondering what Sara wanted—and whether he could accept it or not. When he had decided that it was probably all right, he would carry on. He danced like a ballet dancer and looked as though he had never had so much fun in his life—just until he didn't understand something. Then he stopped. Sara fell head over heels in love with him. When she dismounted she was absolutely agreed with Elisabet. Magic was special and deserved to be properly trained, not just ridden in the forest for fun.

When Sara drove home from the stable that day, she felt really happy for the first time in a long while. She realized that Mozart would be sold, that was an unavoidable fact, but Somebody had sent Elisabet and Magic her way. Sara knew that Somebody or Something was with her and guiding her. In the last year she had sometimes been led to doubt that Good would always conquer. But deep down inside she knew that it would. It was that faith which had helped her through all the difficulties thus far. The knowledge that everything has a deeper meaning than one can see in this life here on earth had always carried her through the difficulties. The fact that she had now got a new horse could naturally not make up for the loss of Mozart, but perhaps it would assuage it a little.

The buyer who wanted to purchase Mozart was a German horse dealer. Admittedly with a good reputation, but nonetheless a horse dealer. It tore at Sara's soul when he accepted her price and wanted to take the horse a few days later. Sara had no choice. Mozart was examined, found to be the picture of good health, and off he went to Germany.

Almost two months later, Sara got a letter from the man who had bought her horse. He wondered when she could come and fetch it? It was lame and had been since he got it, he claimed. Sara was shocked. Mozart lame? What did he mean?

She contacted the German and learned that he wanted his money back, and that she would have to fetch the horse. It had to be done as soon as possible. Sara was desperate. The money was still there but what had the man done to Mozart to make him lame? Mozart, who had never had any problem with any of his legs all the years Sara had had him. They arranged to meet at a veterinary clinic in Germany. Sara drove her car with the trailer to the meeting. When she saw Mozart she thought her heart would break. He stood there with his head hanging down and looking completely apathetic.

'Amadeus!' She almost whispered his name, but he heard her. He lifted his head and whinnied hysterically. She rushed forward to him and threw her arms round his neck. 'My darling, darling Amadeus, can you ever forgive me?' She felt like a traitor as Mozart looked at her with his dark brown eyes. But he seemed just to be happy that she was there.

The vet examined Mozart and found he was lame in three legs! Sara talked to the vet and asked what it was due to. 'Lack of new shoes, poor riding and no love,' he replied. 'So there's nothing seriously wrong with him?' wondered Sara. The vet soothed her fears. If she just took the horse home, he would probably be completely well again in two or three weeks time. So Mozart went home again. Sara gave back the money to the horse dealer. She was furious with herself for selling her horse to him, but it was too late for regrets now. Instead she loaded Mozart into the trailer and began the journey home to Sweden. The vet had been right. After just two weeks, four new shoes and masses of love, Mozart was himself again. But nothing had changed financially, so she was still forced to see whether she could sell him. This time she would make sure that it was to a buyer who was perfect in every respect. A few weeks later Richard came up with a new buyer. He was devastated at the way the horse dealer had behaved and promised Sara that nothing like that would happen again. He told her that the German had evidently bought Mozart because he had a Japanese buyer who was willing to pay three times what he had paid Sara. But for some reason the Japanese had backed out of the deal. The horse dealer had left Mozart standing in the stable without letting him out to get any exercise. When he had then suddenly found a prospective buyer, the horse had been taken out and ridden and then put back in the stable again for a week or longer. Mozart, who was used to being out every day, both when he was ridden and when he was in the field, had naturally not been able to cope with that kind of treatment.

But now he was back in his stable again. He was fit and his coat was gleaming The lady Richard brought with him, Carol Willington, looked thrilled. While she rode Mozart, Richard told Sara a little about her. Sara learned that if she bought the horse, he would have a luxury lifestyle. Carol came from England, where she had her own riding stables. She would have Mozart to ride him herself and learn on. He would have his own field and she guaranteed that he would never be sold again.

Sara realized that Mozart couldn't have a better life. But it was only as she sat and talked to the Englishwoman that she was entirely convinced that she was doing the right thing in selling Mozart to her. She told Sara about her stable and how Mozart would be living. Without boasting she described in glowing terms her stable, the fields and the beautiful surroundings. It was in northern England, just south of Scotland, that this paradise was located, and there Mozart would have his future. Carol Willington wanted to have Mozart as soon as possible. She also wanted Sara to travel with him on the journey, just so that he would feel as contented as possible.

26

Book? Film?

The day of their departure drew closer. Sara had made all her preparations as carefully as she could. It was a long journey for a horse and it was important that nothing should go wrong. She had accepted the idea that she and Mozart had to part. She was glad and grateful that Carol Willington had crossed their path. They had hit it off immediately and Sara had even been able to tell her a little about the real cause of her having to sell Mozart.

Carol had asked Sara to stay a week or so when she came with Mozart, just so that he wouldn't get anxious and start wondering what kind of new place he had landed in. They would be travelling by boat for more than twenty-four hours and then there would be several hours drive even after they had landed in England.

Even though Sara had imagined a fantastic place, that was nothing compared with what met her and Mozart. His new home was up on a hill, high above a big lake and with views into the far distance! It was the most fantastic property you could imagine. The stable looked like a big luxury villa with open half doors for each horse, so that they could stand and look out. The boxes were enormous and classical music was playing from loudspeakers. Sara thought she was in a dream, and it almost looked as though Amadeus thought he had landed in a horses' heaven too!

The foreman of the yard had met them at the ferry station and loaded Mozart on to a big air-conditioned horse transport.

And here was Carol in the stable waiting for them when they arrived. She showed Sara which box Mozart was to have. His name plate was already on it: W. Amadeus Mozart, in gold letters! The days which followed were like a wonderful dream. Sara was able to see that Mozart couldn't have got a better home.

A few days before Sara was to leave, Carol told her about a good friend of hers who happened to be visiting England from the States. Carol had told her friend Samantha about Sara's fate and a little of the unhappy experiences she had just undergone. She had also told her that Sara had memories of an earlier life. Samantha, who was a film producer, had immediately been interested.

In the evening they ate dinner together. Sara talked unreservedly about her life. About her memories from her childhood, her time as a police officer and finally everything that had happened to her over the past year.

'Haven't you ever thought of writing your story down?' Samantha was enthusiastic. She tried to get Sara to see that that was precisely what she should do. Then she should let her, Samantha, have the rights to make a movie. Sara looked in amazement at the woman in front of her. A movie? She couldn't understand how Samantha, a film producer from Hollywood, could be interested in her story. Surely there must be loads of writers in the USA who could write good film scripts?

Well of course there were, but Samantha thought that Sara's story was incredibly fascinating. Not least because it was actually true, even though it was highly improbable in many aspects. What is more, Samantha thought that the message about repeated lives on earth was so significant that it was reason enough in itself to make Sara's story famous. When on top of that she heard the way people carried on in the Swedish police force and in the world of Swedish sport, there was even more reason she thought.

'Promise me you'll write your story,' were the last words Samantha called as she stuck her head out of the car window and drove off. Carol continued her persuasions. Finally Sara promised at least to consider the idea.

When Sara went to say goodbye to Mozart, he stood like a king in his paddock looking out over the neighbourhood. She saw that he looked very contented and happy. He tossed his head in a funny movement, as he had always done when he was loose and happy. And then he trotted off, with his tail high in the air and with dancing steps. He snorted loudly and then charged off over the meadow at full speed.

Sara looked after him for a long time. She was sad that they couldn't be together any more, but in her heart she was delighted with his newfound luxury lifestyle. She would be coming back to see him. She had decided that before she jumped into the waiting car which was to take her to the airport for her flight home.

When she was sitting on the plane the days at Carol's seemed unreal. The wonderful people she had got to know, and everything she had experienced, were a memory which she would carry with her always. Once again, she felt the deep conviction that there was a meaning in everything which had happened. One thing had led to another, and now she sat there and thought about whether she should write and tell people about her life and her memories. But what would people say if she claimed that she had been Anne Frank in her previous life? Was it possible to write in such a way that people would really be able to understand how she had carried these memories with her through life? Could she write about it so that people could and would take it in?

And what would happen if she told them what her life had been like in the Mounted Police division for all those years. How they had treated both her and her horse? The appointment? Could she, did she dare, really tell everything just like it was? It was obvious that if at the same time she claimed that she had lived before, and what's more as Anne Frank, there was every chance that she would be classified as more or less mentally ill.

She was well aware of that, but it was all one and the same thing. If she wrote about the one, she would be compelled to write about the other too. And how could she tell people about her persecutors? Could she really write the true story, just as evil and naked as it was? Sara felt confused, the questions were multiplying. Part of her was completely convinced that this was precisely what she should do, describe the naked truth, just exactly as it was. The other part of her felt uncertainty and fear. Uncertainty of her own ability to write so that people would want to read and understand. Fear that someone or some people would be hurt.

She knew that there were still relatives of Anne Frank living. The last thing she wanted was to cause them any harm. Perhaps they would think that she, Sara, was a fortune hunter at Anne Frank's expense? That must not happen.

After many deliberations this way and that, Sara had decided. She couldn't write her story down. The idea had undoubtedly been a good one on Samantha's side, but it just wasn't possible. And what use would it be? She didn't need to convince anyone who she had been in her previous incarnation. She knew herself and that was enough. Nobody would believe what she had to tell anyway.

27

The other side of hell

Alec and Sara kept in close contact. He told her that he had spoken to the Prosecutor and that the latter had expressed the wish to meet Alec in person to discuss the whole case. This sounded promising, thought Alec. Sara felt hopeful. He also told her that the same day he had been in touch with Bud Mudie of the Riding Federation by phone. Alec had informed him of the pending investigation by the Public Prosecutor's Office. 'I thought they should have a little taste of what you have been put through.'

The next day Alec rang. He was fit to explode. The Prosecutor had informed him that the case had been dropped. He had not provided any explanation for his sudden change of attitude and Alec was absolutely flabbergasted. The Prosecutor had said that they should meet to go through the case together. And now he'd just dropped the whole thing. Not even Alec knew what else they could do to obtain justice.

Sara received the news with a deceptive calm. The Prosecutor had been her last hope. She had pinned all her faith and all her trust on his being a sensible and honest man who would see how unfairly she had been treated, and be appalled by it. Now there was no hope any more. Calmly and matter-of-factly she asked Alec to try and investigate other possibilities.

The days passed and Sara lived as if in a trance. She was there in body but not in mind. She had asked herself countless times why she had had to go through those terrible memories in her constant nightmares. What was it supposed to lead to and what was the meaning of it? Even though she had learned in her dreams what was behind the witch hunt she had been subjected to, she still couldn't have done anything about it. They had succeeded in destroying her very existence and her life once again. In this life they hadn't been able to attack her physically, as they had done in the previous one, but they had still managed to do what they had set out to do—put an end to her.

Her last hope had been for them to be called to account for their actions through the offices of the Prosecutor. Now that he too had deemed that what they had done to her was fully acceptable, she felt that she had no strength left any more. She was ready to give up. She was frightened by her own uncontrollable despair. It washed over her like murky muddy water. She couldn't even cry for help. She carried all the agony inside herself and put on a mask which deceived even her nearest and dearest.

Deep down inside Sara knew that she had to pull herself together if her time on this earth was not to come to an end this time around. She had to bring herself to seek the Force which she knew was deep inside her, and which had helped her through other dark times in her life. Like so many times before, she sought solitude to find an answer to her questions and solace in her bottomless despair. By the sea she sought the strength which she knew was in her.

The experience as a child of meeting the Wanderer on the beach and following in his footsteps was something she had carried with her all her life. He had always, just as He had promised, been there within her whenever she had needed and sought Him. Now she searched desperately for His closeness and perfection. Her life hung on the finest of threads, and she knew that she could only find the answer in her innermost, deepest being.

She wandered barefoot over the smooth rocks, polished by the sea for thousands of years. She followed the flight of the seabirds in the reddening evening sky. Evening after evening she sat and looked out over the sea. She followed the setting sun's union with the horizon. It was only the last glittering rays of the sun which saw the sorrow and loneliness in her eyes. The blood-red disc threw its last gilded reflections across the rippled surface of the water. They reached right to the edge of the rocks, right to her bare feet. As if the sun, with its last, glowing rays, was trying to offer her warmth and comfort.

It was an extraordinary evening. She had sat a long, long time on the edge of the rocks, looking out across the sea. Now the sun had disappeared below the horizon. It had taken with it that glittering golden pathway across the water. Sara got up. Through the darkening twilight she walked slowly home. The gulls had fallen silent and the sea was still. The bare rocks stood out like mysterious statues against the burning horizon.

It was moments like this that Sara had stored in her soul like precious jewels, moments of fellowship and total communion with nature and the Force. As she left the sea and the rocks behind her that evening, it was with fresh spiritual strength. As she sat on the rocks she had been filled with an inner peace and a certainty that everything would be set right. Sara had received the help and the strength she had prayed for so intensely and which were her last hope. But still she did not know how strong that Force was and what doors it would open to her.

That night and many thereafter Sara would return to her previous existence. To the annexe. Not to experience the fear and the terrors, but to get answers to her questions.

She sees herself as Anne and as Sara. The picture changes the whole time. She is sitting at a table writing. It is the same little room which she has seen before in her dreams. But now the helplessness and the fear are no longer surrounding her.

It is with a feeling of indescribable harmony that Sara returns each night to the annexe and writes the story of her life. Of her persecutors. She knows that if she gets the whole truth written down, they will never more be able to hurt her. Only by stripping them down to all their naked evil can she free herself from their spirits and their curses. Once and for all.

But first she must be able to forgive them too and feel sorry for them, in spite of all the ill they have done her. When she could forgive them they would themselves one day be called to account before the Law. She could do nothing about that. She could only free herself from them, and by forgiving them pave the way to a better future for herself as well.

Night after night she returned, and it was always the same picture which guided her. When she woke in the morning she remembered every word she had written in her dream. The dreams by night affected Sara's life by day. Suddenly everything was more bearable. Gradually she became aware that the dreams were giving her answers. Answers to many, many questions.

She was compelled to start writing, not just in her dream but also in the reality of daily consciousness. She was compelled to write down the truth about what had happened to her in this life, and about her memories from the previous one. She had to tell of her persecutors, who in their sick souls had pursued her, not just then but now too—so that she would atone for something they imagined she had been guilty of. Naturally they were unaware of this themselves, but they were nonetheless guilty.

She had to write to release her soul from the fear and terror she had experienced. Then and now. She would leave out nothing. Perhaps she would be mocked or attacked, perhaps nobody would believe her story. But it didn't really matter. She would write simply because she had to. She would rid herself of her terrible memories and her persecutors for good. Never again would they dare to hurt her, or be able to.

Sara realized the risks in relating her memories from her life as Anne. Going out openly and claiming that you had been one of the most talked about people in history wouldn't be easy. But what should she do? She couldn't help remembering. It was not something she could change. Admittedly it would undoubtedly have been better if she had had the memories of a completely unknown girl instead. But she couldn't go and invent something just so as not to upset people.

Perhaps she would be blamed for trying to make money out of the name Anne Frank, but that wasn't something she could do anything about either. She couldn't not tell the story just because she didn't dare to say who she had been. The important thing was not really for people to believe that she really had been Anne in her previous life, but to spread the message of reincarnation. Naturally she had had many previous lives as well, but she didn't remember anything about them at this moment.

What is more she would be leaving a door open for those who wanted to claim that she was just making it up, about the police and the sports world ... That would make it easier for the ones who had been singled out to say, 'But of course it's obvious that she's not really all there, she even thinks she was Anne Frank!'

Sara decided that when her story had been written and was

ready to be published, it should only happen if Anne Frank's surviving relations approved it. Somehow she would make sure that the person or people who were still alive would be allowed to read her story first. Without their consent it would stop there. If the story was published it would mean that the relatives had permitted it to be.

Sara would tell everything just as she had experienced it, then the readers would have to decide for themselves whether they wanted to believe her or not. She felt that it was necessary to try and write so that the reader could understand how important it is to realize, and not deny, the connection between different lives on earth. To realize and accept that there is something before, and that there will be something after the life we live now. And that this connection is far more significant than we can imagine.

Sara knew that there were a lot of people like herself, who had met with different kinds of crisis in their lives, who had been bullied in school or at work, who had to experience indescribable sorrow, who fell into depression—and who finally, as a last resort, had perhaps even considered taking their own lives. She hoped, deep down inside, that her story would help some of these people.

If only she could write about how important, even vital it is never to give up in the face of evil, regardless of how dark and wretched everything may seem. Evil was present on the earth and would probably always be there. It would always try to conquer Good. But the more people there were who believed in Good, and in the Good Force within themselves, the greater the possibility of keeping evil under control. If only they could believe in Good, and in the presence of the inner Force, many unhappy people would be able to fight their way up from the darkness.

When she herself had stood on the very brink of the decision to end her own life, she had desperately sought the Holy
Presence within her. She had found it in the last trembling
minute, just before evil would have overcome her. The Force
which saved her life is there in every human being, evil or
good. But evil people don't seek it, they cling firmly to evil.

Most people on earth were not yet aware that they could
find the Good Force within themselves and that it could help
them if they only sought it out.

Sara realized that a lot of people would laugh at her, many
would perhaps attack her for what she wrote, but that would
only demonstrate where the stronghold of evil and foolishness
really lay. If her story could only help a single unhappy human
being, then it didn't matter whether others mocked or ma-
ligned her.

What Sara had gone through had almost annihilated her.
But she had managed to come out the other side of hell,
stronger and more clear-sighted than ever before.

A poem which she had written many, many years earlier
surfaced in her consciousness:

> You have to go down where the shadows fall
> to possess yourself of the crystals,
> far beyond boundaries which men call knowledge,
> bleeding, you search in the dark.
> When you've gone so far that your feet are bleeding
> and the troubles of the earth can kill,
> then trembling you come to where the light falls
> with your hands overflowing with crystals.

Sara's decision to write was a real turning point. Things

gradually began to fall into place. Her inner strength grew each night that she returned to the annexe–and each day she wrote down what she had seen herself write in her dream.

28

Free!

Sara had not dared to institute legal proceedings against any of her slanderers, since the money she had got for Mozart wouldn't be enough if anything went wrong. She had also seen, with horror, that the term of her leave of absence was rapidly running out. She would be forced to go back, since her financial situation would leave her no other option.

But now something happened which Sara would never have dared to imagine, even in her wildest dreams. One day she got a letter from a solicitor. He informed her that she, Sara, was appointed the sole heir to a lady with whom Sara had corresponded ever since her first book had come out. Now that fine old lady had passed on and Sara was invited to attend the reading of the will.

At first Sara couldn't understand it at all. But it turned out that the old lady had wished with her whole heart to give Sara everything she had to leave. In one single moment Sara's circumstances were completely changed. She didn't need to go back to work as a police officer, and for the time being she would not need to worry about her finances. She could dare to institute legal proceedings to perhaps obtain redress after all. She felt a deep and humble gratitude towards the old lady, who through her generosity and kindness had so radically changed her circumstances.

When Alec heard what had happened he was at first absolutely dumbstruck. When he realized that Sara wasn't joking, he couldn't hold back his delight. 'But dearest child, this means that if you want to you can instigate proceedings against the people who have persecuted you.'

Many, many times Sara had wondered how her persecutors had been able to chalk up one success after another. But now the old truth was confirmed once again: everything is put right sooner or later, just as it should be, if only you have faith and trust in the Good Force.

She thought back to when the persecution had begun in the Mounted Police. Now she found that almost everyone had left under Vernon's and Ulrich's leadership. The atmosphere had become unbearable and now most of the police officers were new. Rose had battled on and, with the support of the new staff and after a lot of ifs and buts, she had been appointed an instructor. But only for dressage training. Vernon and Ulrich were still responsible for the police training. They were still working against Rose as much as they could, but on their own they were not strong enough to harm her.

The poor police horses were an absolute disaster. Out of nineteen horses not even half could be used in traffic. More than once there had been big pictures in the papers of police horses lying in the road after rearing up. People questioned whether the police on their wild horses were not more dangerous than the demonstrators or the football spectators? There was more and more discussion about whether the Mounted Police should be or not be. Sara, who still had a few months left of her leave of absence, decided to hand in her final notice.

As far as Mike and Veronica were concerned, Sara learned that Mike's sister had thrown both of them out. Money had disappeared and Mike had refused to believe his sister when she told him that it was Veronica who was behind it, even though his sister had proof.

One day, Susy Sanders, who was one of the people who had reported Sara for ill-treating the stallion she'd been riding, came by. Suddenly Susy was there in the school where Sara was riding Magic. Her eyes were full of tears and she indicated that she wanted Sara to stop and talk. She told her how Pester had put pressure on her to sign those absurd accusations. 'When Pester realized that I had seen you riding the stallion that day when he was being so difficult, she just wouldn't give up. She was on my back time and time again, putting pressure on me. Finally I gave in and signed the ready-prepared statement. I didn't understand how wrong it was. Everybody was talking about you and how cruel you were.'

Sara really didn't know what to say to Susy. She actually felt rather sorry for her. In all her naivety and stupidity she evidently hadn't known any better.

'Now I've heard that you're thinking of suing the people who reported you, and I'm frightened that might mean me as well.'

When Sara still looked uncomprehendingly at her, she hastened to add: 'I know you are innocent of the charges. I was sitting in the café and saw you walking round and talking to Rita and Steve. But Pester forbade me to say anything.'

Susy looked relieved when she had finished speaking. When she left, Sara stayed where she was, sitting on Magic. The tears fell, not from sorrow, but from relief. She could see the end of her long nightmare. It would take a long time before all the legal enquiries were completed. It would be hard to go through them and it would cost a lot of money. But when it was all over, and her life could go on, she would go on writing and telling people. There was so much more she wanted to write about. So many important things.

When she had gathered her strength, and when she knew how the account she was writing just now had been received by people who read it, she might write a sequel. The most important thing now was to finish the account, the truth about her lives, the previous one and this one.

She wrote and wrote. By night in her dreams, by day in reality. Once again reality and the dream went hand in hand. But now every night and every dream gave her more and more strength.

She doesn't add anything and she doesn't take anything away. She just writes what she sees herself writing in her dream. Night after night she returns. She writes so fast that the pen flies over the paper. The book is reaching its conclusion.

In the dream she sees how she puts a full stop at the end of the last sentence. 'She is free, her soul is free.'

She sees how she gets up from the chair in the annexe. She sees herself leave the room, smiling, with the book in her hand. She goes down the steep staircase which she went down previously in such fear. Now it is with a feeling of complete liberation.

Now they can't hurt her any more. Not as Anne, not as Sara. She is free, her soul is free.

The howling of the wolves has finally stopped.

'What would people say if she claimed that she had been Anne Frank?'

Facts and reflections on some reactions to this book

by Thomas Meyer

Amsterdam, May 1995—or how it all began

Fifty years after the end of World War II in May 1945, the world was full of commemorations of that event. And as 1945 also marked the ending of the systematic slaughter of almost all the Jews of Europe, the *ending of the Holocaust* was commemorated at the same time. Naturally this was accompanied by numerous celebrations and exhibitions about the life and death of its best known victim—Anne Frank. Thus, in May 1995, millions of people were united both in remembering their relief at the end of a horrible war and in a renewal of grief over the demonic murder and tragic destinies of its victims which are as it were symbolized and represented by the life and death of Anne Frank.

Such an international commemoration of a tragic stretch of human history was not unexpected. Indeed, it gave expression to the fact that inhumanity had not won to a degree that could make human beings totally *forget*. What is extraordinary, however, is that among the countless voices of people mourning over the deaths of the victims of World war II in general and of the Holocaust in particular there were also a number that spoke an entirely different language: voices of certain individuals who had experienced how they had gone from death in the Holocaust to a new life in the second part of the twentieth century.

In May 1995 a Dutch television station broadcast a programme which interviewed a number of those individuals who had such very different memories of the Holocaust. Each in his or her own unique way, they told the story of how they had suffered from it, died in it and then found themselves—often while undergoing traumatic experiences during childhood and youth—in a new incarnation.

One of the persons invited to participate in that programme was Barbro Karlén, the author of this book, who was born in Gothenburg in May 1954.[1] It should be noted that Karlén did not put herself forward; she was *asked* to come to Amsterdam at that particular time of May 1995. She herself had never so far publicly spoken about her reincarnation memories as a child and youngster.[2] She 'surprised herself', as she put it in the broadcast, that she had actually consented to come and tell her story in public. So she told the story of her childhood and youth with those memories of another life. She spoke of her visit to Amsterdam at the age of 10 and how she had immediately recognized the city and particular details of the Anne Frank House without ever having been there in this life. This is Sara's story as told in the first chapter of this book.

That Dutch television interview in May 1995 (followed by two public appearances of Karlén in Stuttgart and Basle in October 1995 not directly connected with her reincarnation memories), triggered the writing of the present book and justified its publication, at least in the eyes of the writer of this afterword, who first published it in November 1997 in Basle—the very city where Anne's father Otto Frank had lived and, up to his death in 1980, worked untiringly to spread the message contained in his daughter's diary. Basle is also the place where the world rights of Anne's diary are kept and administered by the Anne Frank-Fonds.

Reactions to the German language publication of Karlén's book in 1997 were unexpected and surprising, in that they were either extremely positive or extremely negative.

Slander and Obstruction

Immediately after publication, a private organization of Holocaust activists launched a fierce attack on the Swiss publishing house, Perseus Verlag, for having published a book with allegedly anti-Semitic and racist contents—six years prior to the publication of Karlén's story.[3] After several months of a public slander campaign the matter was taken up by the Public Prosecutors, and then dropped in May 1998. Shortly before this, two public events involving Barbro Karlén were announced in the press. On those occasions the activists behind the previous attack revealed that their real target was Barbro Karlén and her story. They immediately embarked on a direct disruption of the Karlén forum evenings. Thanks to the decisiveness of Chairman Ronald Goldberger, the planed discussions took place notwithstanding. At the Zurich event, however, various fanatics entered the building and physically attacked several members of the audience. The campaign culminated in calls for the resignation of the president of the Anne Frank-Fonds, for the absurd reason that he refused to publicly refute Barbro Karlén's story. These incidents attracted major media coverage in Switzerland. Some warmly favoured the whole event, others argued that Karlén's 'claims' would belittle the tragedy of the Holocaust and would represent a real offence to its actual victims. One 'prominent Holocaust victim' who started to comment was Binjamin Wilkomirski.

The 'utmost disgust' of Binjamin Wilkomirski

At that time, Wilkomirski was the famous author of some deeply moving Holocaust memoirs which earned their writer worldwide sympathy and admiration, and several awards. His book had first been published in 1995 (by the Jewish department of Suhrkamp in Frankfurt am Main, the home town of the Frank family) the very year when Barbro Karlén and others had first publicly introduced the new spiritual dimension of reincarnation into the whole Holocaust debate.[4] Wilkomirski's book was a bestseller and had been translated into more than a dozen languages. (In English it was published by Schocken Books in 1997 under the title *Fragments: Memories of a Wartime Childhood*.) The author recalls living and miraculously surviving as a little boy in the concentration camps of Maidanek and Auschwitz and, after his rescue, being brought up in Switzerland.

'With utmost disgust, even horror', wrote Wilkomirski in May 1998, 'I have followed the activities by and around Mrs Barbo [sic] Karlén who claims to be the reincarnation of Anne Frank who died in Bergen-Belsen ... To propagate such vaguely-esoteric ideas is like slapping the face of every Holocaust survivor who up to the present day has had to cope with the hard reality of the Holocaust and with the very real consequences for his own life. The direction this reincarnation story is drifting towards is revealed by the horrifying fact that the performances [in Basle and Zurich] are organized in partial collaboration with people responsible for the new edition of the anti-Semitic book *Das Rätsel des Judentums* by Ludwig Thieben ... I welcome and back ... your request for personal consequences. Sincerely, Binjamin Wilkomirski.'[5]

The Jewish writer and journalist Daniel Ganzfried has since alleged to have proven conclusively that Wilkomirski's Holocaust

memoirs are faked. In 1999, CBS and the BBC broadcast doc-
umentaries about this fraud, both based on the investigations of
Ganzfried. The web of lies which had already started to be populated
by other faked Holocaust 'survivors' was destroyed.

Interestingly enough, the impostor Wilkomirski was the *first*
person introduced as an 'authoritative witness' against Barbro Karlén's Holocaust statements.

Simon Wiesenthal or reincarnation as an 'illness'

Wilkomirski's rejection of Karlén's experiences was followed by
some other prominent criticism, this time by someone whose
identity and moral credibility are beyond doubt: Simon Wiesenthal.
After World war II Wiesenthal, who had himself survived the concentration camp of Mauthausen, began tracking down hidden Nazi
officials such as Adolf Eichmann and others. He was also the first to
investigate the background of the betrayal which led to the arrest of
the Frank family in their Amsterdam annex on 4 August 1944. To do
this he sought the cooperation of Otto Frank, Anne's father, and was
surprised to find that Otto Frank had much less interest than himself in tracing and publicly accusing the person who betrayed the
Frank family. It was Wiesenthal who identified the Nazi official who
carried out the arrest: the Austrian Karl Josef Silberbauer. It is
probable that his involvement in these investigations prompted his
comment on Barbro Karlén and her experiences. Wiesenthal wrote:[6]

'Of course I share your concern and your rejection [of Karlén's
memories], for Anne Frank together with her diary is for me a
unique phenomenon in the history of the Shoah. Every attempt to
separate her body from her soul must be rejected; in my opinion
there is no reincarnation—even less so for such persons who claim to
have reincarnated and who can only base this assertion on their own

feelings … Anne Frank and her diary are a symbol with which people can identify. Her life and her dying, her thoughts and feelings which, through her diary, have become known in the whole world have bestowed on her as a victim of an inhuman regime more compassion and sympathy than has ever been directed towards any other person or any other literary document. I do not wish to insinuate any dubious motifs on the part of Mrs Babro [sic] Karlén. If I were a medical practitioner I would certainly be able to make a proper diagnosis of her so called reincarnation. It is known to me that during Catholic processions, for example, which take place each year in Jerusalem, some people turn up who claim to be the reincarnation of Jesus. These persons are sent for medical treatment with the consent of the Catholic church. Sincerely yours, Simon Wiesenthal.'

One might ask what Wiesenthal's wholesale rejection of reincarnation is based on. Has he investigated the case with the same degree of thoroughness that he applied to his investigation of the arrest of the Frank family? His rejection of reincarnation may be understandable, but his proposal of a medical diagnosis and treatment is somewhat disconcerting. It makes it appear as though the man who hunted Nazi criminals, who amongst all sorts of other atrocities performed physical sterilizations to prevent the 'wrong' race from propagating, were in a way advocating another kind of 'sterilization' against the 'wrong' kind of individual experiences, as if *all* of them were just due to some mental insanity or physical disease.[7]

Contradictions—to what?

There was a further category of critics of Karlén's reincarnation statements. They found a number of contradictions between what is actually known (or seems to be known) of the life and dying of Anne Frank and certain descriptions in this book. Some argued, for example, that the description of the arrest scene given at the beginning of this book contradicts certain historical facts. Thus the main protagonist in the arrest of the Frank family (Silberbauer) could not possibly have reincarnated in the nineteen fifties or sixties in Sweden—as the main protagonist of the corresponding scene in the book did—since he was still alive at that time. Furthermore, Sara describes her previous death as one of being burnt alive, whereas it is considered an established fact that Anne Frank and her sister Margot died as the result of a typhoid epidemic in Bergen-Belsen.

But is there no possibility that some of the historical facts may have been incompletely or inaccurately investigated? Or can it perhaps be taken for granted that the reincarnation memory—if it exists—might be more reliable than the physical memory? After all, it would have to encompass a much larger span of time, including even some time not spent on earth. Contradictions or inconsistencies of this kind can certainly not 'prove' that the remembering individual and the one remembered must be two different entities. Nobody would deny the identity of a sixty-year-old man with himself as a five-year-old boy on the grounds that some of his memories contradict those of his brothers or parents or some documents describing his childhood years as that boy.

Even in some circles in which the idea of reincarnation is theoretically accepted this distinction between the identity question and the possibility of memory errors has not been sufficiently clarified. As a result, some people have been led to believe that the mere demonstration of certain inconsistencies between some descriptions in this book and certain historical facts is sufficient to prove the nonidentity of 'Sara' and Anne.

Can a reincarnation statement be positively verified?

Of course, *positive* proofs of the validity of reincarnation statements can not be found as easily as proofs about purely physical things. Let us compare our ordinary consciousness with a large and doorless apartment house, and the world of physical objects and facts with the various pieces of furniture in its numerous apartments. If a group of tenants living in this house all meet from time to time in a particular apartment and sit around a particular table (maybe to discuss the necessity to keep the rent down) nobody will have to prove the actual existence of that table to them. But surely there are things in the house that only one tenant or another can see or be familiar with. How does he prove the existence of such an object to another person? By simply leading the one who asks for such a proof into the apartment or room where this object (maybe a newly acquired original 'Picasso') can actually be seen. All *physical science* can only confine its field of investigation and proof-finding to the space within the walls of the house.

Spiritual facts, however, are by definition not to be found within this building. Thus, their existence can never be proven within the confines of its walls. If you want to prove anything of a non-physical nature you have to leave the house altogether instead of just going from one apartment to another. But to be able to do so requires you to be willing to depart from your ordinary consciousness which is bound to the physical senses and the reasoning faculty based on sense perception. This is a real difficulty for most of the tenants in our house. Some of them may be quite interested in some of the things outside the house, like angels or demonic beings; and perhaps they would even really like to experience them. But then they suddenly fall back into their old thinking habits and ask you to show them these beings somewhere within the walls of the house, perhaps in some very hidden part of it. They sometimes even believe that an object found in a hidden or obscure part (perhaps the cellar) of the house is an 'occult' or 'spiritual' object. Their laziness about getting out of their ordinary consciousness inspires in them this misplaced desire that angels or the immortal human soul or other super-sensible beings must be as solid and tangible as tables and chairs. In other words: they want the same type of proof for things both inside and outside the walls of their house. But they do not actually want to step outside it.

There *are* natural ways to step outside. One of them is normally rather unconscious, namely the step we take every night by going to sleep. We actually sleep 'outside the house' of our bodily con-sciousness. Unfortunately most of us are not strong enough or trained enough to remain conscious beyond some rather dim degree while outside. 'Unfortunately', because outside the house there is for 'the seer' an abundance of supersensible or spiritual facts and beings whose existence is proven to him by supersensible perception, just as the existence of the table is proven by physical sight. Some people spontaneously wake up while outside the house during sleep. They become spontaneous 'seers'. They have conscious out-of-body experiences and bring the memories of them back through 'the walls of forgetfulness' into their apartment in the house. (Some of the experiences of Sara Carpenter are of this kind.) Others choose to go the active way of conscious training, and study in their waking consciousness the nature of the walls, thus discovering that there are means to stay awake and yet penetrate them (in complete mental sanity, unlike the 'Jesus-reincarnations' of Jerusalem ...) and get outside the house.

This is the way of *spiritual science*. On the basis of the education of a sound reasoning faculty (and other exercises) it leads the spiritual individuality of man out of the walls of his bodily consciousness on to a higher plane of experience. Only on such a higher plane of experience can the strictly spiritual-scientific proof for concrete reincarnation statements be found.

Looking at symptoms

Between a naive belief (or disbelief) in reincarnation statements and a spiritual-scientific proof of their validity or invalidity there is a middle realm that can act like a bridge between the two: This is the *symptomatic observation* of certain elements within human life. For in the house described above their are, as it were, certain *signs* or *arrows* on some of the floors or walls that seem to point to certain spiritual elements outside the house. Such elements can be grasped by unbiased thinking, long before they may one day be actually experienced. Even if you are not able or not willing yet really to leave the doorless house, you can take these signs seriously and start to interpret certain things and happenings within the house in terms of elements which in their full reality can only be met outside.

Such symptomatic signs can be found in the whole description 'Sara Carpenter' gives of her first visit to Amsterdam; of her feeling of having no immediate need for a new name; of her dislike of certain foods; of the fact that she does not mind what others think or say about her story and so on. Anyone with an unbiased openness and a certain sense of discrimination can undertake the task of reading such signs. Of course, we can also prefer to look at them briefly, pass on and leave them unexplained. In this case we do not *read*. Even if such reading gives no full supersensible proof as yet, it is a safe first step for developing the faculty of 'stepping outside' to see for oneself...

Some of the negative reactions mentioned above may also be

valuable for a symptomatic assessment of Karlén's past life statements. They all seem to have some things in common: They represent the attempt to prove or insinuate the non-existence of something outside the house by going up and down in one of its rooms or studying the wallpaper. They show a tendency to make authoritative assertions about things that have not been thoroughly investigated and which some of the critics even claim cannot be investigated by the human mind. These critics display either a more emotional or a more intellectual irritation about the fact of Karlén's utterances.

The combination of these three factors can lead us to the question: Well, why then such a public ado about all this 'fabrication' and 'illusion'? Why this amount of smoke? Is it the fire of a deeper truth that some people are dimly aware of while they may be afraid that it might burn down their piles of prejudices? Is that why such attempts are being made to smother this fire? Before turning to look briefly at what we consider to be a real 'fire element' in this book, we should like to point out that there have, of course, also been some very positive media reactions.

Rabbi Yonassan Gershom—a Hasidic view on Karlén

In spring 1999 the magazine *Life and Soul* published an article on Barbro Karlén by Rabbi Yonassan Gershom. Gershom, an orthodox Hasidic teacher and writer, had introduced the reincarnation perspective into the Holocaust discussion with the publication of his book *Beyond the Ashes* (1992) and *From Ashes to Healing* (1996). He shows how reincarnation has always been accepted and taught by the Hasidic stream of Judaism. In his books he tells the story of how he met—or was rather found by—many people with troubling memories which often turned out to be Holocaust reincarnation memories. Though each and every case may not be equally convincing to the reader, his case reports deserve to be taken seriously. They add in their own way to the necessary counterweight over against the one sided tendencies to consider the Holocaust merely in moral, political, financial or purely emotional terms.

Regarding Barbro Karlén's experiences, Gershom carefully notes the various symptoms in the early life of Sara Carpenter that seem to be pointing to a reality. 'For my part I do not doubt Karlén's sincerity. I am even willing to believe that she was killed by the Nazis in another life', he writes. But as he wishes to go beyond symptoms to actual proofs, he asks for 'some solid documentation' and explains: 'It is a given that the reader is going to want further proof'.

But what is a 'proof' in spiritual matters? Whoever does not make a clear distinction between symptom and proof in such cases is likely to overlook the fact that—unlike the verifying symptoms referred to also by Gershom—actual proofs for spiritual experience can *never* be found *within* the doorless house mentioned above. In other words, they are not to be looked for on the physical plane but *within a higher spiritual consciousness*. Gershom concludes his remarkable article by stating: 'The jury is still out.' We should like to add: Excellent! But if this jury is not only to judge the validity of spiritual experience by reading symptoms, but by actually proving (or disproving) their inner reality, it must be composed of individuals who are able to leave the house of ordinary consciousness. Otherwise their verdict will be of no avail.

A voice from the *International Herald Tribune*

In autumn 1998 *The International Herald Tribune* published in its English language magazine supplement *Ha'aretz* the following comments: 'Those who read Karlén's book with an unjaundiced eye will find what may appear to be a surprising answer: Not only does her reincarnation revive the unspeakable atrocities of the Holocaust period, but it turns the experiences of her present life into a direct outgrowth of them. Karlén is reliving the barbarity of those times, in an altered form, of course, but her perceptions of the horror are so keen that the subhuman deeds of the Nazis almost come alive. Thus the notion that souls are reborn does not diminish the horrors of the Holocaust. It intensifies them and doubles their heinousness. For that reason, and out of respect for those who perished, this book deserves to be taken seriously ... Barbro Karlén ends many of her interviews with the same remark: "It does not matter to me whether or not people believe I lived as Anne Frank. I know that I did, and for me, that is sufficient. What is important to me is that people understand my message about the profundity of life. That is what will give them the strength and hope to cope with whatever ordeals they must face." '

Those who seriously look for a symptomatic evaluation of Karlén's book will be able to find quite a number of essential points within this unusually open and unbiased review.[8]

The fiery truth of reincarnation

At the very core of this book is a personal statement of reincarnation and the precise workings of the laws of destiny (karma). There were serious attempts at the beginning of this century to elaborate both within the context of a new spiritual science which was meant to complement the physical science of our time. Thus Rudolf Steiner, the founder of spiritual science, tried to introduce the old truths of reincarnation and karma in a modern spiritual-scientific form into western culture. Had this been taken up in Central Europe no Holocaust could ever have happened. For one of the foremost implications of reincarnation is that the indestructible core of every human being passes, in the course of its various incarnations, through various male or female bodies belonging to various *different races*. The permanent individuality itself is superior to any single race, while all of the races and peoples are there to provide it with ever new possibilities for its unfoldment. You cannot accept the truth of reincarnation and be a racist or fanatical nationalist at the same time. On the contrary: the more reincarnation is taken seriously, the more true interest and respect for all races and peoples of this earth can develop. If the soul or individuality of man incarnates now in one race, now in another, now in this people, now in that, how can we possibly rank one race or one people above the others? A real understanding and experience of reincarnation may indeed prove to be the strongest and most radical cure for the widespread pathological tendencies appearing in all sorts of 'racisms' or 'nationalisms'.

Unfortunately, at the beginning of this century German culture, or rather what was left of it, was unable and unwilling to lift itself to the level of such a spiritualization. Instead—and because of this lack—it produced the Holocaust. It is not without deeper significance that now, at the end of the century, it is precisely through some of the victims of the Holocaust that the fiery truths of reincarnation and karma are being brought back to Western humanity for a second time within a century. Whilst most Germans and Europeans scornfully rejected this truth when it was presented to them in spiritual-scientific terms at the beginning of the twentieth century, it is to be hoped that *after* the Holocaust they may start to accept it in its new form: born out of terrible individual experiences of suffering and death. Anne Frank's life has become a world-wide synonym for the ruthless annihilation of flourishing human life. Barbro Karlén's

life gives an example of the indestructibility of the individuality-core within each human personality. Her message complements that of Anne Frank. It shows that despite all the atrocities of the 'Final Solution' the life and further development of the human individuality can never be halted. The fire that burnt Sara in her past life could not extinguish the eternal core of her individuality in which the fiery truth of reincarnation has awakened.

Even if this first English edition were to be met with similar hateful reactions as was the case with the first German edition, no harm will be done. Indeed, it might instead contribute to the awakening of more and more souls to the basic truths presented by this book. In the end all the wolves of the world will be howling in vain against the indestructibility of the spirit-core of every human being.

1 The text of the Karlén interview of this programme was first published in English by *Der Europäer*, Jg. 1, Nr. 8, June 1997. See also on the Internet: http://www.perseus.ch.

2 However, the Swedish magazine *Min Värld* of February 1978 had without permission published an article about the past life statements of Karlén known up to that point only to her family and closest circle of friends.

3 *Das Rätsel des Judentums* (The Riddle of Judaism) by the Jewish-Austrian author Ludwig Thieben. For the identity of the attackers see Note 6. One of the persons seduced to testify in a very general form against an 'anti-Semitic' book which he can hardly have read was the late Ignatz Bubis, former president of the Central Council of Jews of Germany

4 The reincarnation dimension of the Holocaust was first introduced in literary form in 1992 by Rabbi Yonassan Gershom. See page 247.

5 Internet letter faxed to Perseus Verlag. Translated into English by T. Meyer.

6 Wiesenthal (as well as Wilkomirski) was asked for his comments by the 'Aktion Kinder des Holocaust' (Action Children of the Holocaust), a small private organization from which prominent Jewish personalities have openly distanced themselves and which Daniel Ganzfried called an 'obscure organization' (*Die Weltwoche*, 4 November 1999). Wiesenthal's letter, dated 6 June 1998, was faxed to Perseus Verlag and translated into English by T.Meyer. One question to ask is: Who financed the activities of this 'obscure organization'?

7 Of course some 'spiritual' ('reincarnation') experiences do have to be explained in terms of mental or physical illness. A future spiritual medicine freed from one sided-materialism will have to investigate every single case on its merits.

8 See *International Herald Tribune*, 18 September 1998. Another benevolent review, by the Jewish writer Dennis Eisenberg, appeared in *The Jerusalem Post* on 19 March 1999.

ALSO FROM CLAIRVIEW

PSYCHIC WARRIOR
The true story of the CIA's paranormal espionage
programme
David Morehouse

When David Morehouse—a much decorated army officer—was hit by a stray bullet, he began to be plagued with visions and uncontrolled out-of-body experiences. As a consequence, he was recruited as a psychic spy for STARGATE, a highly-classified programme of espionage instigated by the CIA and the US Defence Department. Trained to develop spiritual, clairvoyant capacities, he became one of a select band of 'remote viewers' in pursuit of previously unattainable political and military secrets.

When Morehouse discovered that the next step in the top-secret programme was 'remote influencing'—turning 'viewers' like himself into deadly weapons—he rebelled. In his efforts to expose the programme, he and his family endured the full force of the US intelligence community's attempts to silence him. As the multi-million-dollar STARGATE scandal was exposed to the world, Morehouse himself became the enemy of the secret services...

In *Psychic Warrior*, one of STARGATE's 'viewers' finally reveals the extraordinary truth of this secret operation.

£9.95; 280pp (8 b/w plates); ISBN 1 902636 20 1

MY DESCENT INTO DEATH
and the message of love which brought me back
Howard Storm

'For twenty years, I have been listening to and reading innumerable accounts of near-death experiences, but I have rarely encountered one as powerful as Howard Storm's'—Dr Kenneth Ring, author of *Lessons from the Light*.

'... I consider Howard Storm's near death experience one of the greatest that I am aware of ... I highly recommend this book.'—George Ritchie, author of *Return from Tomorrow* and *Ordered to Return*.

For years Howard Storm lived the American dream. He had a fine home, a family, and a successful career as an art professor and painter. Then, without warning, he found himself in hospital in excruciating pain, awaiting an emergency operation. He realized with horror that his death was a real possibility.

Storm was totally unprepared for what was to happen next. He found himself out of his body, staring at his own physical form. But this was no hallucination; he was fully aware and felt more alive than ever before. In his spirit form, Storm was drawn into fearsome realms of darkness and death, where he experienced the terrible consequences of a life of selfishness and materialism. However, his journey also took him into regions of light where he conversed with angelic beings and the Lord of Light Himself, who sent him back to earth with a message of love.

My Descent into Death is Howard Storm's full story: from his near death experience in Paris to his full recovery back home in the United States, and the subsequent transformation of his life. Storm also communicates what he learned in his conversations with heavenly spiritual beings, revealing how the world will be in the future, the real meaning of life, what happens when we die, the role of angels, and much more. What he has to say will challenge those who believe that human awareness ends with death.

£8.95; 184pp (8 b/w plates); 1 902636 16 3

SEVEN STEPS TO ETERNITY
The true story of one man's journey into the afterlife
as told to 'psychic surgeon' Stephen Turoff

'I died in the Battle of the Somme...' These were the astonishing first
words spoken to clairvoyant and healer Stephen Turoff by the soul
of James Legett, a soldier who was killed in the First World War. For
two years, the world famous 'psychic surgeon' communicated with
the soldier's soul, and in the process wrote down his remarkable
story; not the tale of Legett's tragically short life on the physical
plane, but of his death on a battlefield in France and his soul's
subsequent journey into the afterlife.

Although he works with many discarnate spirits in his clinic, the
dyslexic Turoff was initially reluctant to undertake the task of
writing a book. But he was persuaded by the boisterous and genial
soul of the dead man. Their literary collaboration involved an
unusual method: Legett presented spiritual pictures to Turoff, who
with clairvoyant perception interpreted them into words. The result
is this enlightening testimony of life beyond the illusion of death,
filled with insight, spiritual wisdom and delightful humour. It is
written to show that we are all eternal; there is no death... only
change.

'One of the best books of this genre to cross my desk in some time;
its easy style will be of equal appeal to experienced readers and
newcomers to spiritual matters alike.'—*Psychic News*

£8.95; 192pp; 1 902636 17 1

LIGHT BEYOND THE DARKNESS
How I healed my suicide son after his death
Doré Deverell

'This book is the best I have ever seen for people who have suffered through having a member of their family committing suicide.'—George Ritchie, author of *Return from Tomorrow* and *Ordered to Return*.

Doré Deverell's son Richard had led a difficult life, plagued by physical and mental illness and depression. When he committed suicide at the age of 36, Doré was naturally devastated, suffering the intense anguish of a mother's loss. But she was determined to search for healing and reconciliation.

This book is the first-hand account of how Doré Deverell made contact with Richard after his death. Encountering the work of the spiritual teacher Rudolf Steiner, she discovered unique methods by which she could communicate with her son's spirit. Suicides, she learned, often experience great suffering and regret as a consequence of their premature death. But Doré was taught how to help alleviate Richard's pain, and finally metamorphose it. These practical steps are described in an accessible way to aid anybody who finds themselves in a similar tragic situation.

In the unexpected conclusion to this extraordinary tale, Doré finds the person who, she believes, embodies Richard's reincarnated soul. Her work is rewarded with new hope, and Richard's soul is given a chance to learn and develop on earth once again.

Light Beyond the Darkness is a gripping account of love, despair, death and resurrection. Its central message—that, through the spirit, light overcomes dark—is a heartwarming confirmation of spiritual reality.

£8.95; 144pp; 1 902636 19 8